The History and Practice of Woodcarving

The Author

Frederick Oughton   *The Author*

Derek Gabriel   *The Photographer*
Roger Parmiter   *The Artist*

The History and Practice of

WOOD
CARVING

Stobart & Son Ltd, London

Woodcraft Supply Corporation, Woburn, Mass.

Books by Frederick Oughton

Creative Crafts — *Teach Yourself Series*
Joinery — *Teach Yourself Series*
Primitive Art — *Teach Yourself Series*
A Guide to Woodworking Tools
The Finishing & Refinishing of Woods
Wood Technology

© 1969 Frederick Oughton

This Edition Published April 1976

ISBN 0 85442 005 3

Stobart & Son Ltd, 67–73 Worship Street, London, EC2A 2EL

Woodcraft Supply Corporation, 313 Montvale Avenue, Woburn, Mass. 01801

Printed in Great Britain by Clarke, Doble & Brendon Ltd, of Plymouth and bound by Webb, Son & Co Ltd, at Ferndale

Contents

List of Illustrations

Dedication

For Rhian, my wife, who has often contributed to my carvings, swept up
all the wood shavings, rooted around on the Gower beaches for driftwood,
and allowed the things I have carved to become part of our life together.
   And to Simpson, a mouse, for watching.

With love,
Frederick

Thank you . . .

. . . . to my late stepfather, Joseph Lawton, who steadfastly refused to allow me to handle tools throughout my childhood, thereby stemming a fire which might have burned itself out by now, but instead made me into a carver of wood in my middle years.

. . . to my mother, Daisy, who wanted a carving of her own and forced me to do some practical work when I did not feel like it.

. . . to Ian Arthur and John Elsley, the bookshop men who fired me and forced me to start carving more intensively.

. . . to Derek Gabriel for remaining calm while we wrestled with photographic problems connected with this book; also to Roger Parmiter for coming into it as third man and artist.

. . . to the carvers who have allowed me to show photographs of their work.

. . . to Rhian, my wife, who put up with it when other women would have fled, screaming.

The Author

Foreword

Hold a piece of wood and lay your hand on it. You will feel a soft warmth which will remain locked within it for centuries. Wood is organic. Even when the tree is chopped down and the wood is shaped, it remains alive, meaningful. The wood carver seeks to enhance this life by creating beauty and utilizing grain and texture. And then he imparts the final finish and stands back to look at it, and the wood has a new life.

Wood is one of the original materials of mankind. The tree provided shade from the weather, it gave heat when it was burned, and it donated food in the shape of berries and fruit. Man began to shape his first furniture from it. One anonymous man took a tool and discovered that wood could be patterned or fashioned into shapes. The first man became a carver.

Carving is three things – transformation, transfiguration and preservation.

1

The Barbaric Art

Not long ago I noticed a reader's letter in a woodwork magazine. The writer was a woodwork teacher in a primary school, and he said that while he was a proficient carver, he always lacked ideas to pass on to his pupils. Yet another teacher, who read the preliminary outline of this book for the publisher, thought that in many cases the wood itself must dictate shape, form and design.

Two teachers with two different opinions. But who was right? The problem is not at all simple, but it is one which must be understood and tackled by anybody who carves or teaches carving. As a carver who has from time to time imposed shape and form on the wood, and at other times allowed the wood to do most of the dictating, I think that both viewpoints are right. Loosely speaking, it is right to assume that relief carving will accept your direction, but wood sculpture – that is, carving 'in the round' – will tell you what its final form is to be. But whether you carve in relief or in the round, it is unlikely that you will ever achieve complete self-satisfaction in the act of creation. It is one of the peculiarities of carving that the finished piece should look better than it is.

This book is built around the ideas I have just expressed, and in this it differs radically from many other works on the same subject. The reader will quickly discover that once he has acquired the essentials of tool manipulation and a knowledge of wood, the idea is to start venturing forth. Although carving is a traditional craft and one of the oldest, it still offers freedom of expression. An American carver acquaintance of mine says that in carving the end must justify the means, and he put a match to petrol by being the first man to use power tools for carving. The results were quite unlike any hand-carved work, but on the other hand they showed qualities which could not be obtained by the use of hand tools.

As in painting and all the arts, there are many different methods of carving. Henry Moore probably has a vast array of tools in comparison with a backstreet Hong Kong carver who makes do with a ground-down table knife, but both have something to offer, and if their work has beauty, why worry?

Where the teaching of carving is concerned, young carvers should be left to their own devices, not hamstrung by mentally cramping 'projects' devised by someone else and imposed in such a way as to produce a number of more or less exact copies of the same test design. That kind of marshalling accomplishes nothing. Carving has its own freedom, and it is an intensely personal relationship with the wood. It is a private matter, like a love affair, and the outsider is unwelcome, whether the carver is seven or seventy.

Of course, a child in class must be started off with the basic tools before he can start to experiment on his own account. While the present book tends to range over a selection of alternative methods not only in carving but also in finishing, I have to admit that I myself am something of a purist and probably as opinionated as the rest, although this has never prevented the exploration of new ways of carving, using new tools. Somehow you always come back to the kind of tool which has been in use for centuries.

Obviously, readers who are faced with the job of teaching young people how to carve wood will face a number of problems. The modern addiction to gimmicks, gadgets and the yearning for quick results can over-ride the slow progress of the traditional carver. It is easy enough to permit youngsters to take the easy way out, but at the same time there is always a dividend in creating and stimulating an interest in the traditional tools, if only to show that their effect on wood cannot be reproduced by modern devices. I knew one teacher who 'took wood carving', and he issued his boys with a patent knife and interchangeable blades, then told them to get on with it. In no time he was digging into the first aid box to bandage up all those cut fingers. None of the lads showed future interest in carving. Of course, the reason for this wholesale failure was that the teacher confused American wood whittling with formal carving, and the two are different. But the damage was done, and it typifies what can happen, though fortunately a more enlightened approach is spreading through the schools.

For years I have had doubts that you can teach wood carving beyond a certain definite point, and ultimately you feel like crying with Gauguin: 'If you cannot express yourself properly, talk like a savage, but say something, anything at all . . . It's barbaric, but it's art.' (C'est sauvage, mais c'est de l'art.) This is one of my reasons for dwelling to some extent on primitive art, because it is a starting point in its simplicity, and from it we can develop our own forms and style.

You can show people how to hold the tools, select the wood, make the cuts and so on, but sooner or later student and teacher reach a parting of the ways, and the student who has a genuine creative urge will be impelled to commence his own explorations. And a certain number of students will come to a halt, because sheer copying quickly palls. One of the reasons for this is that wood carving is up against the past. Too many carvers go on creating traditional figures and forms without really expressing themselves. They are more interested in sheer technique than in cultivating the inner eye. Admittedly, a beginner must serve a self-inflicted or a teacher-orientated apprenticeship, and it may well be that tradition will dominate this phase, but stagnation is bound to set in if he fails to study other subjects which may act as mental springboards for original design. You find very few carvers who experiment with themes, as in painting, and you do not find any parallel with, say, Impressionism. Although the standard of modern carving is high, there is no doubt that the archaic atmosphere in which it exists has done practically nothing to keep it alive in a spirit of growth. In the main, we have gone on producing replicas of past carvers who, in turn, were capable only of producing replicas of past carvings.

Despite what looks like a dreary picture, I believe that we may now be heading for a breakthrough. More students in our art schools are turning to carving, particularly in the furniture departments. In the United States several healthy clashes with tradition have occurred, and contemporary carving is now edging into the avant-garde galleries. On the Continent carvers are beginning to blazon wood sculpture as an art form in its own right.

But what about the individual reason for carving? I can do no better than quote the authority of Dr Paul Jaeger of Munich: 'If you have ever made anything with your own hands (poiein the Greeks called it, and they knew it to be closely connected with the divine in us) – even if it was only a toy for your child, or in war-time, when nothing was to be had for a present, perhaps a mere wooden spoon for your wife – you will recall a sense of achievement and the pleasure of those moments and your deep satisfaction over the object you made. It was something of yourself, the fruit of your ingenuity and affection, shaped by your own hands; something made in the image of your own soul – even so trifling a thing as a wooden spoon. And be sure of this: when stricken by grief for some lost paradise – an experience we surely all have at times – you would do well to take a piece of wood or a lump of clay and fashion something with your hands or with a knife. Then distress may turn to satisfaction.'

Let me explain my own position in all this, because it will help the reader to understand why I left my carver's bench to write the present book. I am not an idealist, nor do I believe in sentiment when it comes to craft work, but I will lead the applause for Dr Jaeger's opinion. I applaud even louder when I hear that more art school students are attending carving and wood sculpture classes. In schools I want to see the younger people receiving a good grounding in the craft, but not as a sideline to 'woodwork'. Carving is very much a subject in its own right, and I dislike the idea, which many people have, of it being 'precious'. It should be thought of as everyday stuff.

The majority of pieces I carve are designed to ornament the home. I have discovered that people who would not give a Picasso or a Braque houseroom will be absolutely fascinated by a carving to hang on the wall, regardless of the fact that the carving is more abstract than Picasso or Braque ever knew how to be. One reason for this is that wood is organic, and most of us have a deep affinity with it. We enjoy looking at the grain, the colour and the way it has been shaped. However abstract a carving may be, it generally looks quite at home in the boardroom or the parlour, and I know one case of a petite carving which lives in a lavatory. When you have mastered the business of how to use carving tools and are capable of imparting a proper finish to the wood, try the experiment of taking a piece of pine planking. Cut practically any amoebic shape out of it (see Plate 1), polish it or finish the surface in any way that takes your fancy, then hang it on the wall. Then wait. Some homespun critics may well ask: 'What is it?' and others will demand: 'What does it do?' but as a home-made objet d'art it will soon begin to exert its own fascination. This is just a starting point, a quick experiment, but it is capable of infinite variation.

My own metier happens to be wall decoration, and I find it significant that we can now buy many excellent veneers which are bonded to a base and sold as wall decor instead of paint or wallpaper. Kitchens are faced with imitation planking. Many wallpapers are printed in a grainy wood facsimile. All this suggests a hankering for wood, the basic material which man has used for thousands of years. Perhaps the plastic honeymoon is over at last.

Wall decoration is a matter of taste, yet it embraces many different tastes. It is surprising that you can carve a mask, using a traditional folk design as a starting point, and then embellish it, changing the shape and imparting your own individual 'trademark' with every slice of the gouge. Although you were inspired by an existing mask, you will end up with something which is completely different – the only one of its kind in the world. There is something refreshing and exhilarating in that thought, because you can never completely duplicate a carving. Each one is unique. That probably explains why it appeals to so many of us. Put it down to ego – or a reaction against the times in which we are forced to live.

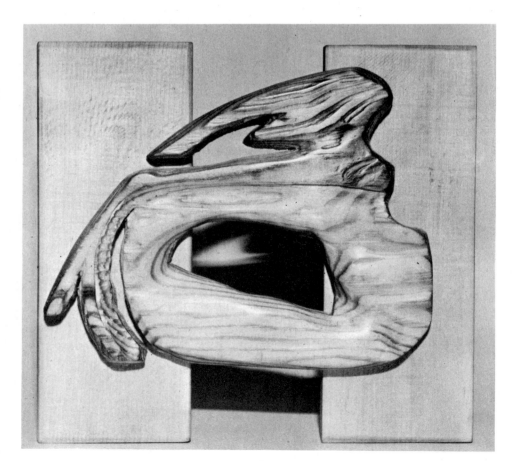

1   The 'amoeba' design by the author, done in pine and mounted on two pieces of lime. Overall dimensions: 10 in.×9 in. The abstract shape to the fore was soaked for twenty-four hours in boiled linseed oil, then lightly waxed. The supporting blocks were slightly polished. Although the design started out as pure abstract, it evolved rapidly into a hare-like figure as a result of following the figuring of the pine. The 'head' (top right) was heavily resinous, suggesting the sleek fur of the animal. Despite the figurative association, this carving can be viewed from several different angles (try it upside down!) and it then becomes other things. Photograph by Derek Gabriel.

2 *Eskimo Mask by the author. This was done very quickly, and while it differs very little in dimension from the original walrus bone creation, it nevertheless has a different personality, enhanced by the addition of metal rods for the eyes. While it is the kind of carving a child can do, it is nevertheless capable of infinite sophistication and variation. Pine. 6½ in. × 5½ in. Oil polished. Photograph by Derek Gabriel.*

Throughout this book you will find examples of what I call 'extended design' or 'the springboard principle'. A notable one is the Eskimo mask (Plates 2, 2A–G), which I first came across in the form of a photograph in an art magazine.

Eskimo art is interesting. It comes from a race numbering only 50,000 (1950 census), which adheres to a spiritual interpretation of the universe with a sky deity, Sila. Most of their art comes from leisure activity, often manifesting itself in bone carvings, because wood is scarce. The mask which took my eye consisted of four bones fastened together with a tapered piece for the nose and a curved mouth drilled into the lower section. My first experiment was to create a parallel in wood (see Plate 2), using a section sawn from a plank. There was very little carving to it. For some obscure reason I later added two vertical aluminium rods to the eyes, and this created a personality effect. The finish was a slight staining of the wood to bring out the pine figuring, followed by three applications of thin shellac. After several weeks of living with the mask, I decided to carve another one, just to see how much primitive ornamentation it would stand. Halfway through the job, I altered the nature of the eyes and the chin section. This resulted in a dissolving of the Eskimo character and what emerged was a suggestion of the Oceanic culture (see Plate 2A). Even when they are placed side by side, the two masks do not suggest a common parentage.

2A *Mask by the author. Another variation, but given a certain amount of ornamentation which makes it Oceanic and suggestive of a Pacific culture. The eyes were altered and cut down in geometric planes. Greater use was made of lighting possibilities, and the figuring of the wood plays a major part. Pine. 11 in.×10½ in. Stained and oil finished. Photograph by Derek Gabriel.*

If you grant your imagination full play, the mainspring of design is unlimited in its energy. The Eskimo mask grew longer, based on the idea of compression or elongation (see Plate 2B), and I began to see something of the Inca culture in it with the *flambeaux* of the sun at top and bottom. This was very difficult to carve, because the irregular *flambeaux* called for riffling.

I somehow do not think that I have seen the end of that Eskimo mask. It has started to design itself, (see drawings 2C–2G), and in a new phase is multiplying in the form of a pierced perspective carving verging on the abstract and owing nothing to any culture.

In the pages that follow I want to treat carving in two phases. The first phase will consider carving in relief, which is my own inclination. One of the advantages of relief carving is that lighting enhances it, another is that most of us have more wall space than floor space. A well-placed relief carving looks much more striking than a dimensional one. Let's face it, if we are to think of carving as a natural everyday function – the kind of thing you can do on one end of the kitchen table – then everything you do should be put to some kind of use, and what better than original domestic ornamentation

in an age when too many 'bought' things are stuffed into too many same-looking semis? A lot of people buy reproductions of paintings, but how many of them ever have a shot at painting for themselves? Similarly, the man – or woman – who does a wood carving and hangs it on the wall will feel a deeper satisfaction than if he goes out and buys a set of plaster ducks or a pseudo antique for the lounge. Plaster ducks and phoney antiques are produced by the million, but this is not a good reason for buying them. There is, however, a perfectly good reason for doing your own carving. It is because you are you.

In the second part of the book we shall be looking at dimensional carving. More correctly, this should be called wood sculpture, because you treat the block of wood in much the same way as the sculptor treats his marble or stone. It obviously represents a second and more complex development for the carver, although I do not want to be arbitrary about this and suggest that dimensional work *must* come later. If you want to experiment, go ahead. As I said previously, carving is a new freedom.

23

2C

R.P.

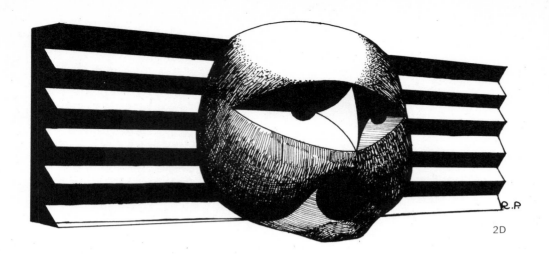

2D

R.P.

2E

R.P.

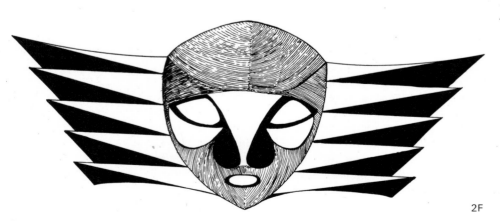

2F

24

These drawings suggest possible extensions of the Eskimo Mask, devised by the author and drawn by Roger Parmiter. It will be seen that the design can be given a sinister appearance, as in 'C' and 'F', and sophistication imparted, as in 'D' and 'E'. It can also be grouped in variations, as in 'G' for wall decoration or embodied in a screen. It is not intended that the reader shall slavishly copy these designs but rather appreciate what is possible, granted a little imagination.

2G

R·P.

Before we embark on the adventure, I want to make a simple and definitive statement – carving is good for you. It is also good for youngsters and the millions of people who are searching for a means of expressing themselves. Although it has so many applications, it remains one of the delightfully lonely activities which can shut out a world which is fast becoming far too crowded with people, noise, and gaudy counters packed full of articles which are produced at the push of a button. When you do a little sweating and cussing, and the only battle is between you and a piece of beautiful wood, then things do start looking better. In fairness, let me add that when the tools move through the wood as through soap or cheese, and the grain comes up under elbow grease and polish – well, that's the stuff heaven is made of.

To quote Karl Hils, a leading German teacher of crafts: 'Craft work is guided by an inner impulse – something derived from play – and it is a manual art that promotes the development of the complete or integrated person. It is distinguished on the one hand from a 'regulated' trade craft and on the other from an aimless finicking labour or an arid manual skill. The skilled trade crafts, manufactures and techniques have at all times grown out of handicrafts. Wherever the craft tool has become a machine, man has abdicated part of his creative freedom.

'Craft-work involves a process of shaping or forming. The zest and spark of creative joy are just as characteristic of it as they are of the happy singing and dancing of natural man, of which he is hardly conscious, and for whom it may be a need, a liberation or even a fulfilment and a release from inner tension. Thus, composing, constructing, answer to some inner need, some psychic compulsion, the expression of which is true to nature, authentic, and convincing. The making of an object in accordance with nature must, necessarily, be the early stage of the skilled trade, which must also include and keep alive all those early virtues, even when it has to be governed by utility and ulterior purpose.'*

It is significant that carving is perhaps the only craft which has not been subjugated by the machine.

* Karl Hils: *Crafts For All*. Routledge and Kegan Paul. 1960.

2

Two Hundred Logs of Ebony— the History of Carving

One almost convincing line of deduction suggests that Jesus of Nazareth was not a carpenter as we understand the term, because in his time wood was very scarce. It seems more logical to think of him as a wood carver. If there is anything in this theory, then we wood carvers have a most impressive lineage.

What we do know with some certainty is that Neolithic Man carved amber, and about 2300 B.C. a carver created a steer-like creature out of bone in what is now Mesopotamia.

In Biblical times Nebuchadnezzar was buried in a mulberry wood coffin, and Solomon built a temple . . . 'And the decoration of the house within was carved with knops and open flowers . . . and he carved all the walls of the house round about with carved figures of cherubims and palm trees and open flowers within and without.' (1 Kings 6: 18, 29.)

As we know, wood was very precious in ancient times. Ebony, a difficult and often recalcitrant material which always seems to be having an argument with your tools, was carried to Tyre prior to 1000 B.C. (Exod. 27: 15), and there it was carved into ceremonial articles, statues and wine cups. Two hundred logs of ebony were sent to Persia every three years by the Ethiopians in tribute – a handsome gift indeed!

During these early times the carver used chisels which were very similar to our own chisels, and he handled a mallet of about the same shape and weight as we now use, also drills, hone, awl, knife, a small hatchet used for trimming the wood before carving it, saws, a plane so like our own as makes no difference, and measuring instruments such as rule and line. It is interesting to compare these tools with the contents of a wood carver's chest of 1500 years *earlier*. This contained chisels fitted with wooden handles, a saw, drills, rasp and oilstone. In a period totalling 3400 years practically nothing happened to alter the shape and the function of the carver's tools. Historical notes on early tools can be found in Section Three: *Tools and a Place to Work.*

The influence of Ancient Greece remains widespread throughout all the arts, but if we want to discover how these influences came through to wood carving, then it is logical to study Greek sculpture. The Greeks used wood as a base for inlays of precious metals, ivory and ebony, and their work is described by Lucian, Arrian, Livy and Pausanias (*circa* 480–400 B.C.). Statues of Jupiter made of wood and decorated with precious metals were sent from Greece to Rome and Pompeii. Corinth and Athens were the principal craft centres.

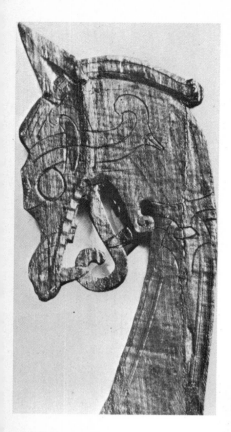

3   This striking and lively head of a horse once graced the prow of a Viking vessel.

4   The main door of Rochefort-en-Terre, Brittany. Weathering has unfortunately worn the detail smooth, but it remains a prime example of early fourteenth-century carving.
Photograph: Feher by courtesy of the French Government Tourist Office.

We now reach a very odd period, for there occurs a gap of about 200 years after the Crucifixion, and the craft seems to have come to a full stop. No reason for this is apparent, but we do know that a renaissance of sorts occurred in Scandinavia about the 9th or 10th century. Carved pine framings have survived, and it is interesting to note that they approximate to Celtic stone crosses in their motifs. Some of the earliest carving of this time is in low relief, the designs being of interlacing stems and some foliage with monstrous near-human heads.

5   *The carved screen in Metz Cathedral – a fine example of richly ornamented medieval craftsmanship. Photograph: Karquel by courtesy of the French Government Tourist Office.*

Although carving lapsed for two centuries, it is certain that the carvers of Asia Minor, China, India and Persia pursued the craft, and the same designs are still perpetuated today in an unbroken tradition.

Not until the eleventh century did carving really spring to life in Northern Europe with Germany as the hub. This was the result of generous church patronage, and the best religious carvings were installed in the great churches and cathedrals of Berlin, Nuremberg, Vienna, Königsberg, Mannheim and Dresden. Carvers of the time used such common woods as chestnut and oak taken from the unspoiled German forests. But after a time, when the patronage and support lessened, and the churches had a surfeit of statuary, screens and ceilings, the carvers had to look elsewhere for a living, and they found it in the homes of wealthy merchants and private patrons.

The records for this particular period are not too reliable, but we do know that Tilmann Riemenschneider, who lived from 1460 to 1531 and came to Würzburg from his home in the Harz Mountains in 1483, was the most accomplished of the craftsmen. From being a working carver with a sale for his work only within the Tauber Valley, he grew to fame. Dealers were soon obtaining high sums for his work throughout Europe. Today his 'Blood Altar' which is preserved in Jacob's Church, Rothenburg, is considered to be one of the best carvings of the period.

English carving was most certainly influenced by the German craftsmen, including Dürer, who is now more famous for his woodcuts, Veit, Stoss, Pacher, Wohlgemuth, Bruggemann and Multscher. The stimulation of the Germans was added to by carvings from Belgium and Holland which found their way into the country. Soon Westminster, the cathedrals at Durham, Canterbury, Gloucester, Exeter and York, and the Collegiate Church of St Stephen, Westminster, were rivalling Germany. All this occurred between 1377 and 1399, when Richard II was on the throne, but a much finer flowering was to come when Queen Elizabeth I ruled England.

What can be called the Early English Period endured for only a century, from 1190 to 1310, and it is unfortunate that the only truly representative example remaining is found in the stalls at Winchester Cathedral. They are remarkable in that the carver outdid the stone-mason, cutting them from solid blocks of oak. Lesser and perhaps more inferior examples of the same period are found at Exeter. Much of this is foliated carving with leaves springing from thick stems. One of the finest examples is in Wells Cathedral.

By the end of the thirteenth century the work of the carvers was increasingly sought after for English church decoration, and examples are to be found in the groined roof with carved bosses at Warmington, Northamptonshire, the carved roof beams at Bradfield, Berkshire, and the moulded beams of Rochester cathedral.

From 1300 to 1370 carving went into what we now call the Decorated Style with distinct characteristics. For instance, foliation became exaggerated, although the treatment of leaf surfaces remained conventional.

The golden age came in the fifteenth century, when the Gothic style prevailed with the Perpendicular style in architecture. Due to the affluence of the age, merchants were able to hire the foremost carvers to decorate their houses both inside and outside. Churches competed, one against the other, to include carvings. One noticeable factor was that carving became flatter, and there was a departure from the habit of cutting screens from solid pieces of oak. The new method was to build up a tracery on separate boards, and then put the boards together. Elsewhere, carving became rich in ornament and decoration, often incorporating religious fables in series of panels.

If Tilmann Riemenschneider was the emperor of German wood carvers, then Grinling Gibbons (1648–1721) was the English king of the craft. He was kept busy with Sir Christopher Wren's commissions while working on carvings for Canterbury Cathedral, Cambridge University and Windsor Castle. Gibbons was a genius of mixed Dutch and English blood, and he was the friend of many famous people, including Pepys and Evelyn, the diarists, but it was Horace Walpole who wrote of him: 'There is no instance of a man before Gibbons who gave to wood the loose and airy lightness of flowers, and chained together the various productions of the elements with a free disorder, natural to each species.' This elegantly sums up Gibbons' work, for he carved fruit, lace, birds, flowers and foliage in such a way that they no longer resembled wood, but were so completely natural that viewers sometimes tried to pluck them from their settings. Much of his work is in panel form, but he also carved pieces which can be seen in St Paul's (foliage and festoons in the choir), St James's (baptismal font), All Hallows, Kensington, and the Archbishop's Throne at Canterbury. He also carried out a great deal of work for Burleigh, Chatsworth and many other fine houses. When he was appointed a master carver in 1714 by George I he became so busy that he had to take on apprentices and assistants to help with his larger creations. One of the wonders of the age was 'The Crucifixion', based on Tintoretto's painting. The carving contained more than a hundred figures. By the time he died Gibbons was the most famous carver of his time, and today his work is still renowned throughout the world.

6 *A typical example of the carving of Grinling Gibbons. The overmantel in the first salon at Cullen House. Photograph by courtesy of the British Travel Association.*

While Gibbons worked in England the Continental carvers created the panels at Les Célestins, Paris, the walnut gates of Aix Cathedral, the Sainte-Chapelle de Vincennes decorations, and they made separate pieces for many houses in Rouen in addition to decorating the exteriors.

Beyond France, in Spain and Portugal, a number of influences, including Moorish and French, were at work, but it was Italy, with the patronage of the Church of Rome, which became the main centre. Representative work is hard to define, because there is so much of it, but we might choose the choir carved by Brunelleschi for the Capanello del Duomo in Florence (early fifteenth century), although it was unfortunately replaced with work of a vastly inferior character in 1547, carver mercifully unknown. The leading figure of the period was Benedetto da Majano, although the great Michelangelo was also known as a carver, and he fashioned the crucifix for the Monastery of San Spirito in 1493, also the cornice of the Farnese Palace in Rome. The carving line grew strong with the addition of Jacopo Tatti, Francesco of Volterra, Domenico Tibaldi and Giovanni Fiammingo.

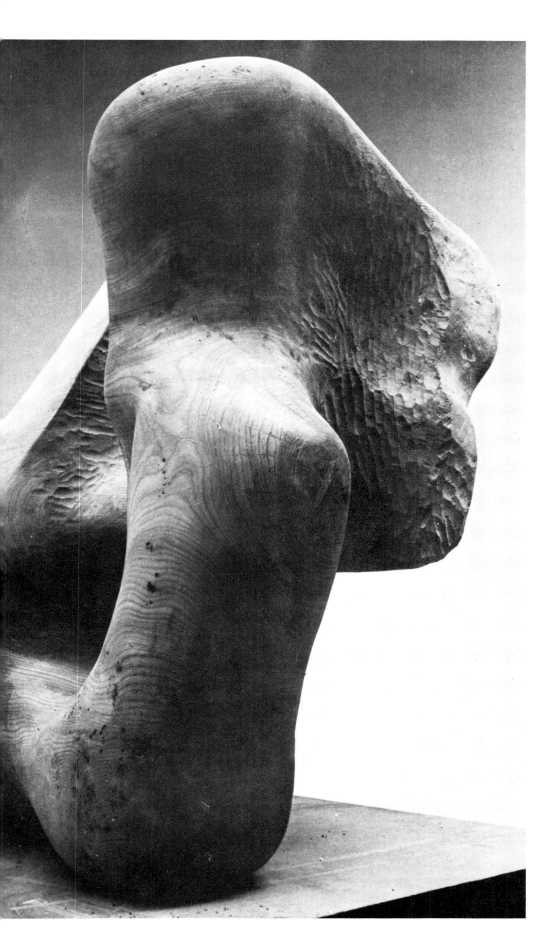

7 'Reclining Figure' by Henry Moore. Elm. 90 in. Photograph by Henry Moore.

For many years Oberammergau has been the European centre of classical carving, and it maintains what we might call a medieval tradition. Carvers have been educated here since 1835, when more than 200 families in the region practised the craft. At the present time about 1000 carvers are being trained. Of these many will become commercial carvers, living on commissions in different parts of the world, and about one quarter of them will depart from the Oberammergau tradition to explore their own acts of creation.

Reverting to the main stream of history, when it looked as though carving might easily die out, it was the furniture industry which came to the rescue and put new life into the craft. The furniture of the Italian Renaissance was notable for its fine carved decoration, and the motifs include the acanthus design with caryatids. Between 1450 and 1585 furniture carving became a major industry. From 1483 onwards French carvers were decorating armoires and cupboards, and this Gallic trend crossed the Channel to England during the reign of Louis XV, where it was taken up by Chippendale, and, later, by Robert Adam, Sheraton and Hepplewhite, who brought to carving a touch of lightness which helped to relieve the original Continental baroque.

By about 1840 carving was again in decline, and while a lot of decorative house carving was still being done, the motifs and designs were generally weak and ineffectual imitations of Grinling Gibbons. Be that as it may, carving did flourish under the hands of journeyman carvers and their apprentices, and much domestic ornamentation was executed at prices which made the art available to more people than ever before. Apart from the domestic carvers there were also coach carvers, specializing in the representation of Cupids, a mass of floriation and festoons and near-classical material. But we have to admit that the coach carving was not much better than the domestic variety, because it was generally lacking the perspective which hallmarked Grinling Gibbons' work. The carvers themselves were improvident fellows, most of them dead drunk when not working. At the pursuit of their craft they worked quickly and were able to earn as much as four pounds a week throughout the year – a wage which put them amongst the affluent in the London of the eighteenth century. Even the ordinary journeyman carver could count on making a wage of between thirty shillings and two pounds a week, and he was seldom unemployed for long. But as far as the standard of carving was concerned, this was poor. A contemporary account (quoted from *The London Tradesman* by R. Campbell, 1747) says: 'The carving now used is but the outlines of the art, it consists only in some unmeaning scroll, or a bad representation of some fruit or flowers. The gentry, because it is the mode, will have some sort of carving, but are no judges of the execution of the work: they bargain with the master-builder or architect for something of the kind; he, to make the most of it, employs such hands as can give him a slight flourish for his money, no matter how it is done, therefore it is not necessary to spend much time or money to acquire this superficial kind of carving.'

In the United States the English influence crept in, but the inclination was to favour the French style, and some of this was taken up by Duncan Phyfe, who decorated mahogany with brass. It is debatable whether American carving has any native basis except the style known as Colonial and Spanish Mission, but even here the motifs are adaptations of foreign schools of carving.

The situation today is changing – or it seems to be. In the furniture departments of art schools and colleges it is possible to find carving classes engaged on brave new experiments, although attempts to create a fresh and untrammelled style are thwarted to some extent, because modern furniture does not lend itself to decoration, and the accent is on severe line.

The modern scene is divided into two parts, for carvers are also studying their art in sculpture classes, creating dimensional free-standing pieces which often have a startling originality. Here, at least, wood is a medium in its own right, stimulated to a great extent by sculptors of the standing of Henry Moore (see Plate 7).

It is realized that moves could be made at an earlier stage of education to create special areas of study and whet the appetites of young people, for there is a chance here of building a new generation of wood carvers. But what is lacking in many teachers at this level is a knowledge of form and design. The use of the tools is quite easily taught. Encouragement to experiment is another matter. Something can be learned from history. Architects, builders and carvers were responsible for the Middle Ages revival, and it is from a study of the methods of these men that we can learn a great deal if we want to give young people a chance. While working as a team, the cathedral builders remained individualists, and the imprint of each craftsman was plain to see, especially in carving. It is a paradox that the contemporary interpretation of teamwork means a certain subordination of the personality. Yet in the Middle Ages each member of the team was a strong individual. Teachers nowadays can use the craft structure of that time when young people are working together, and it should be possible to design group projects.

3

Tools and a Place to Work

Man the tool maker first created tools in order to make things, and then he began to ornament his habitations and carve idols. In many instances the tools themselves and fragments of ornamentation are our only clues to early history. Man has never been able to exist at a solely biological level. He is impelled to create, utilize and beautify. After clay and pebbles, his first material was wood, and he made wooden tools. Later came iron, and then steel.

The best material for carving tools is tempered steel. In order to maintain them throughout their working lives, it is helpful to know something about their properties. Many a would-be carver new to the business has attempted the disastrous experiment of heating a gouge, chisel, fluter or veiner in the flame of a blowlamp in the belief that this will further temper the steel and improve the cutting edge. Even the slightest knowledge of metallurgy will tell you that tempering steel is a highly skilled job and most definitely not one for any carver. The steel is already at the best temper for its purpose when it is fashioned for you by the tool maker.

Although there are several variations in the lengths of carving tools – long, short and medium with certain intermediates – their function remains the same. Some stockists supply them without ash or maple handles, others come complete with handles. The handles themselves are precision turned with rings cut into their circumference, or they come in a mushroom shape. Slim tapered handles are best suited for work with the mallet, while the mushroom shape, which fits snugly into the palm of the hand, is good for close intricate work, because the cutting end projects only slightly beyond the fingers, giving maximum control. You should not use a mallet against a mushroom handle, because its length makes it unsuitable, and you are likely to give your fingers a crippling blow.

When you buy your handles separately you have the job of fixing the tools into them. This is not at all difficult. All you have to do is protect the tool itself with a cloth wrapping, and then close the vice jaws on it so that the spiked end to enter the wooden handle protrudes. The spike, or tang, should be inserted in the hole, which has been drilled by the maker. Press down firmly, and then adopt a twisting action. This should go on until about one inch of tang remains. Now use the mallet to tap it home. If this is done properly, it will stay put forever.

In use, carving tools should be like an extension of the arm and hand. They should never feel cumbersome or prove difficult to control, even when you are working in a restricted position, but it will take a few practice runs before you get the true 'feel' of them. This applies more specifically to the long tools, which have an overall length of about 11 in., including the handle. At first it will be like working with a spade or shovel, but confidence comes quickly. Some carvers – especially young people – take time to get used to the longer, heavier tools, especially if they have been trained on mushroom handles, and it is advisable to devote equal time to both. As you might expect, the big tools are intended for large, bold work, although they are also useful for the preliminary bosting-in of comparatively small work.

About fifty per cent of the effectiveness of a carving tool consists of the use of the wrist muscles. It is not necessarily the fingers, the grip of the palm of the hand or the hand itself which controls the tool, it is the wrist. Even if you happen to have weak wrists, you will find that carving strengthens these particular muscles.

A word about tool handles. If you do have to buy them, choose round ash or maple ones, because they are hard and they should sustain many heavy blows from the mallet without splitting. Handles come in four sizes to match tool sizes, and they are generally sold by the inch. An average sized carving consists of many thousands of cuts, both bold and small, simple and complicated, and these are made in part with the tool and mallet blows. It takes ash or maple to withstand such rugged treatment. Lesser woods will split, splinter or else go mushy at the business end, and a handle which does this will reduce your efficiency, quite apart from the fact that it will not transmit the mallet blows in a predictable manner. When you begin to use a mallet, you quickly get to know what the effect of different blows will be on the tool and on the wood itself.

On pages 38–48 you will find illustrations showing the different carving tools. Tempted by such an array, many beginners want to take out their cheque books and immediately buy everything in sight. Being able to do so must be wonderful, but it is not necessarily conducive to good carving. Rather the reverse. Teachers who want to show young people how to carve are well advised to confine them to the basic tools, and I would recommend

Henry Taylor's 'Acorn' brand. The wood carving tool sets which are offered by reputable makers contain the bare essentials. For instance, one standard set contains the following:

$\frac{1}{2}$ in. (13 mm.) chisel
$\frac{5}{8}$ in. (16 mm.) chisel
$\frac{3}{4}$ in. (19 mm.) gouge
$\frac{1}{2}$ in. (13 mm.) gouge
$\frac{3}{8}$ in. ($9\frac{1}{2}$ mm.) chisel
$\frac{1}{4}$ in. ($6\frac{1}{2}$ mm.) gouge

This can be later augmented and the following tools added:

$\frac{3}{8}$ in. ($9\frac{1}{2}$ mm.) corner chisel
$\frac{1}{8}$ in. (3 mm.) gouge
$\frac{3}{16}$ in. (5 mm.) chisel
$\frac{1}{4}$ in. ($6\frac{1}{2}$ mm.) gouge (backbent or curved)
$\frac{1}{4}$ in. ($6\frac{1}{2}$ mm.) parting tool

The following tools can be acquired at a later stage:

Macaroni – $\frac{1}{4}$ in., $\frac{6}{16}$ in., $\frac{1}{2}$ in.
Backeroni – $\frac{1}{4}$ in., $\frac{6}{16}$ in., $\frac{1}{2}$ in.
Fluteroni – $\frac{1}{4}$ in., $\frac{6}{16}$ in., $\frac{1}{2}$ in.

Conventional wood-working tools which have some occasional use include a coping saw, crosscut saw (26 in.), screwdriver (14 in. blade), brace and bit, rose countersink bit, hand brace, try square, steel rule, bow saw and wing compasses and other drawing instruments.

8   Twenty-seven basic wood carving tools. Although this looks like a formidable array, I generally find myself using only three or four on a job. The photograph also shows the top of the Sjoberg workbench with the useful trough at the back. It is useful for shavings and chips, and it also holds tools safely.
Photographer: Derek Gabriel

The wood carver's mallet, which has been mentioned, is bell-shaped and short-handled, and it comes in four different sizes and weights – the professional (11 in. long × 30 oz), the student (10 in. long × 16 oz), the amateur (7 in. long × 7–14 oz) and the Old English (8 in. long × 12–24 oz). They are made from beech or lignum vitae, the latter being the hardest known wood apart from snakewood. The so-called 'half-weight' mallet of 14 oz is useful for delicate work, especially if you are so new to carving that you find it difficult to gauge with any accuracy the effects of a blow. The lighter mallet is a form of insurance against the damage which can be done by the ham-fisted – and most of us suffer from this complaint when we start carving, although young people are generally better at it than adults, who start off by regarding the wood as an enemy rather than a friend.

It is all very well preaching about restricting yourself on tools, but I am a compulsive buyer, and my own tool chest is a comfortable jumble of things which have only occasional uses. It contains all kinds of odds and ends of tools, most of them unused from one year to the next, because I always come back to a small range. It is rather like having too many friends when you want to be part of a small intimate circle.

All the tools you use have a long history. Drills, for instance, go back to 3000 B.C. At Saqqara about 2540 B.C. an elaborate drill stock was in use, and proof of this exists in a relief panel where the craftsman is shown using it. The Greeks and the Romans used the same kind of tool, but the bow drill went out of use after the Roman era, and breast plates were introduced, probably because they were much faster.

My own ratchet drill is an adaptation of the bow drill. It is sufficiently well designed to hold a selection of drills in the hollow handle, and these range from the delicate $\frac{5}{64}$ in. to $\frac{7}{64}$ in., $\frac{9}{64}$ in. and the comparatively large $\frac{11}{64}$ in. Together, this quartet meet most of my requirements whether I am working on small or large carvings. I use the drills when I am operating on restricted internal surfaces, especially for pierced carving, because if you can bore a hole and then apply a coping saw or a fretsaw, the wood is removed in moments, and this saves a great deal of gouging and puffing and blowing. It does no harm to impart such tricks of the trade to young carvers, because it can save boredom.

An alternative to the ratchet drill is the hand drill which operates by crank action and is geared so that each crank turns the drill three times, which is about the best ratio to avoid overheating of the drill itself if the right speed is maintained. Hand drills of this sort go up to $\frac{1}{4}$ in., and getting it started entails digging a small hole in the wood with an awl.

Breast drills are a larger version of the hand drill, **and** they use drills up to $\frac{1}{2}$ in. They are fitted with a curved breast plate which **is** placed in the small of the shoulder to give pressure during drilling.

The awl, which I mentioned above, is a useful general utility tool in carving, because apart from its capacity for making holes, it will also make guide lines on the wood. You can use it to sever awkward pieces of wood in tight corners.

I mentioned the saw in connection with pierced carving. Sawing of this sort must not be overdone, otherwise you may as well take up fretwork, but there is nothing against the compass saw with its long tapering blade, the coping saw, the keyhole saw and the fretsaw, although fretsaws seem to dislike dealing with thick wood and they often snap angrily if forced to work too hard. Another saw is available, made principally for modellers, and it can be quite useful for small work, because the blade is only $1\frac{1}{2}$ in. long. Another one is the saw knife with interchangeable blades. But the trouble with small saws is that they bend very easily, whereas a good steel chisel

9   *The woodcarver's mallet, bell-shaped and short handled, should be well balanced, made from beech or lignum vitae, weighing between 14 and 30 oz. Selecting one is a matter of preference, but the 14 oz model is recommended for beginners.*

will often do the same job very cleanly with a couple of cuts.

Like other tools, saws have a history. Flint saws were found in La Madeleine Cave in the River Vézère Valley in Southern France, and they date back 37,000 years. In 450 B.C. metal saws were in use in Northern Italy and Switzerland. When the Royal hearse graves, about 3,000 years old, were opened at Kish, near Ur of the Chaldees in Mesopotamia, some metal-bladed saws were discovered. But it should be added that the modern saw with its precision-cut teeth is a different proposition, altogether more accurate than its ancient forebears.

The carver will also use a plane to correct edges, to smooth surfaces. Planes were found in the ruins of Pompeii, and this dates them prior to A.D. 79. Pliny the Elder wrote about them as follows: 'The shavings of this wood [fir], when briskly planed, curl up in circles, like the tendrils of the vine.' I remember when browsing around the Egyptian Museum in Cairo seeing the stock of a rounding plane with the iron fixed into it – a method still in use in the eighteenth century.

Carvers often use the small jack plane, which dates back to 50 B.C., when the Romans made them out of wood. The metal-bodied plane of modern times dates back to 1827. Varieties used by carvers include the block plane, which is approximately 6 in. long and has a plane angle unique among these tools. It is so called because it is used for blocking in. The smooth plane is 7 in. to 10 in. long with the plane iron bevel mounted down, and it is used to smooth rough surfaces. The jack plane, also called the jackass, because it has a general utility, is 12 in. to 15 in. long with an extra length for edge-straightening. Fore and jointer planes are 18 in. to 24 in. long and share the characteristics of the jack plane. The scrub plane is 9 in. to 10 in. long with a rounded cutting edge which will quickly reduce the wood. And lastly there is the handy baby of the plane family, called a miniature model plane, and used by violin makers. It is only $3\frac{1}{2}$ in. long with a steeply inclined blade.

Cleaning up the surface of the wood before you start marking out and carving is one of the tedious things which just has to be done. Removal of the top surface accomplishes two things. It provides a smoother face on which the design may be pencilled in, and it also coaxes out some of the figuring which will help you to assess the way the various facets of the final carving should fall.

Revealing the surface can also be done with a sander, although it often leaves granules of abrasive behind, and these do your tools no good. It is rapid, efficient, noisy and it covers you in a fine dust. The plane, on the other hand, makes a happy zizzing sound as it tackles the job.

Another tool worth a place on top of the bench and not in the drawer is the wood rasp, 8 in., 10 in. and 12 in., which belongs to the file family. He is a singularly tough person and will attack any sort of wood with his sharp teeth.

The classification of files follows what is known as the Swiss Pattern. No. 00 is the coarsest, then Nos. 0, 1, 2, 3, 4 and 6 become progressively finer.

I prefer to use a file without a handle, because more control seems possible over its movement and the effect on the wood. (Careful, though! The tang can pierce the palm of the hand if used injudiciously.) My favourite file has four working surfaces; one side is half-rounded and divided into coarse and medium, the other side being flat and with the same abrasive qualities. It is $9\frac{3}{4}$ in. long and 1 in. wide.

Your first attempt to use a rasp or a coarse file may surprise you, because if any pressure at all is used, great areas of wood can be speedily shifted, especially when you are reducing any edges. Obviously, a lot depends on pressure, but you can also use a feather touch with interesting results. This is a tool with many uses, but it is at its best when roughing out edges.

The only other file I use with any frequency is a rat-tail. It is rounded with a fine cut and very useful for smoothing down internal cut-out shapes. A variation of this is the mouse-tail, about the thickness of wire and conveniently pliable.

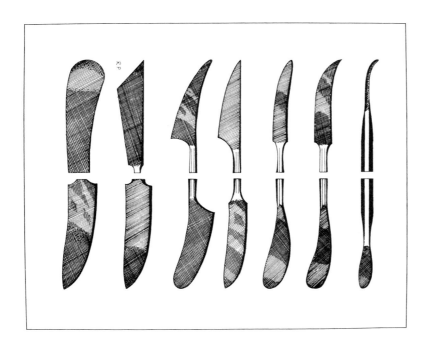

10 *Rifflers: maids-of-all-work to the carver. They are supplied in three different lengths with proportionately sized heads, the biggest being 12 in. Their proportions are very suitable for getting into those difficult and almost inaccessible places in a detailed carving. They also help you to create curves in the toughest wood.*

Rifflers are files of a sort, but files with a difference; they are maids-of-all-work because of their variety of shapes – see above. They are good things to have on the bench when you are working on small figures, floriation and concave and convex surfaces. It is possible to buy rifflers of Italian manufacture in eight different shapes, each of which is available in five sizes, 6 in., 7 in., 8 in., and 12 in., all of medium cut. They are comparatively inexpensive, because they have a long life and do so many awkward jobs for you. Rifflers are not sold by ordinary hardware dealers, but are obtained from dealers who specialize in sculptors' and carvers' equipment.

There has always been a lot of argument about the use of sandpaper in carving.* The anti-abrasive brigade claim that all it does is soften the distinctive lines of a carving and remove the tool marks which, for some obscure reason, are supposed to increase the aesthetic value of the finished piece. Naturally, a lot must depend on the carving itself, but in many cases it is better to bring out the figuring so that the medium itself plays a role in the aesthetic appeal. It would seem that the anti-abrasive brigade want to revert to the custom of the medieval carvers, who seldom bothered to finish and polish a carving but merely rubbed a handful of workshop shavings over it. No doubt they were pressed by the need to start the next commission and make some money.

* There is even argument as to what you call it! Probably the most 'correct' term is Cabinet paper, but I stick unrepentantly to sandpaper.

11 *These drawings of wood carving tools illustrate the wide diversity of cuts possible. Most of these are available in different sizes and backbent or straight. They are made from forged steel, and beechwood handles can be bought separately.*

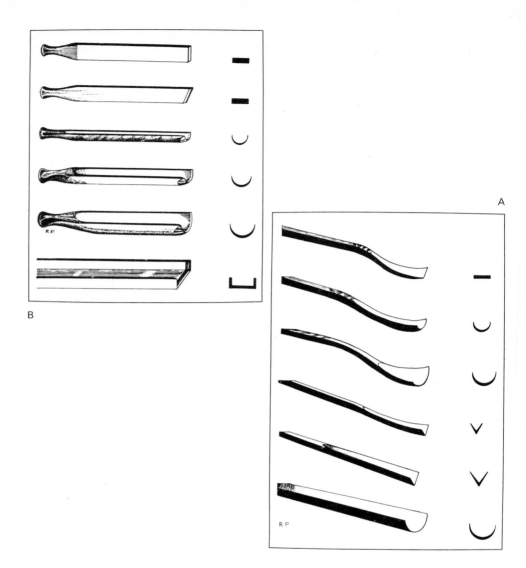

Nowadays we can do fuller justice to the figuring of the wood, not only by the use of garnet and sandpaper but also a series of interesting finishes and polishes which were not available to the medieval carver. These are explained in Section Ten: *Finishing*. In the end, it is your own choice, and taste is your only guide.

The abrasive is mentioned in the Old Testament, the reference being to *shamir*, a stone. Today we identify it as emery, and the modern name is after Cape Emeri on the island of Naxos, Greece, where it is still mined in large quantities. As a definite product emery cloth originated in the thirteenth century, and it was first made by the Chinese, who used a natural gum to stick fragmented seashells on to parchment. But manufacture ceased until two hundred years ago, when the Swiss reintroduced a similar product made by sticking powdered glass on paper. This was a complete failure, the glass being too soft to do anything more than scratch and spoil the wood. The next development was a mixture of crushed flint and gemstone called garnet. Then a final innovation resulted from experiments to manufacture commercial diamonds by heating a mixture of silica and carbon at a temperature of 4,000°F. The result was not diamonds but silica-carbon, and this remains our hardest abrasive, also the basis of the better brands of paper used by the wood carver.

If you want the best results from sandpaper you just have to experiment, and the beginner should buy as wide a selection as possible. Some stores sell a selection as a kind of package deal. Glass paper can be used on wood with a pronounced grain, also for rounded carvings. A warning: whatever you use, it should be rubbed with the grain, never across it, otherwise you will scratch the wood, and to get rid of the marks you may have to re-cut the surface.

Now for the important consideration of a place to work. The first benches, made back in antiquity, were ordinary trestles, but later a plank was laid between two trestles and the bench was born. The carver sat astride it to keep the workpiece steady. Benches designed by the Romans were copied and used in the Middle Ages.

As a rule schools will have no trouble in establishing a carving department, because most of them already possess a woodworking department equipped with long, firm benches and the usual ancillary bench equipment. But sooner or later some of the young people may want to do some carving at home. Everything depends on the mentality of parents, but if a youngster evinces the desire, then he should be given the chance on the understanding that he cleans up his own shavings. This applies also to adults who want to carve. I am a bit of a hypocrite in saying this, because more often than not my wife is good enough to clean up after me – an exceptional girl she is in that respect.

Parents who think that television shows and record players provide sufficient entertainment for youngsters may do posterity a favour if they can manage to allocate some kitchen table space to the tyro, bearing in mind that carving can be a noisy business.

When you boil it down, the basic requirement of 'a place to work' is simple enough. All you need is a firm surface. Your tools can be kept wrapped up in a piece of baize or coarse linen, or stowed away under the bed in an old shoe box. But the surface you work on must be firm enough not to shake or even shiver when you start using that mallet. It should be long enough and wide enough to accommodate both work and tools with space for manipulation of the workpiece.

But if you want to make a bench for yourself, here are the suggested dimensions: it should be 5 ft long and between 2 ft and 2 ft 6 in. wide with a height of 3 ft to 3 ft 6 in. The legs should be cross-stressed, and the top about two inches thick.

It is a good idea to use a stool of comfortable height for long spells at the bench, and if you are working from drawings or diagrams, they should be pinned up on the wall over the bench for constant reference.

During the last few years I seem to have carved on a wide variety of surfaces, but even the most makeshift ones have never detracted from the job in hand. I used to clamp my work to the surface of a desk where I still do my writing, and while some people may frown at the numerous scars and cuts which now mar the polished surface, I treasure them because they are reminders of work completed. Another of my work-sites was a small kitchen table . . . and I have often carved with the wood held firm between my knees, although I do not recommend this to the beginner, because a chisel in the kneecap can be quite painful.

At present I work on a Sjoberg B. S. 122 bench (shown on Plate 12) which is finished to such a high degree that it could easily take up its position in a drawing-room without offending the purist. Sjoberg benches of various shapes and sizes are made from beech and fir with pine trestle work. Mine has an arrangement of vices and bench-dogs which enable you to hold even very large work stable under the most rigorous mallet blows.

12 This photograph shows the commodious drawers and cupboard, and the left-hand holding vice which are part of the Sjoberg workbench. Photographer: Derek Gabriel

13 Four cramps of different sizes and uses, an awl and the useful wood rasp. Photographer: Derek Gabriel

14 Some of the smaller workpieces can be comfortably held in a bench vice with a flat piece of wood as a protective facing. In this photograph I am beginning to carve a Tudor figure 9 in high. Photographer: Derek Gabriel

The bench-dogs are not unlike the bench stops used by the Romans. As to the Sjoberg bench itself, I was recently interested to discover that the design was outlined by Loffelholz in 1505 in Nuremberg. But two centuries were to go by before this system of vices was put to use.

My bench has five drawers, one with a separator for small tools and odds and ends, and a large cupboard. The top is generously proportioned with a trough for holding tools and shavings. I think I should add that the makers of the Sjoberg in Sweden do not pay me for being generous in its praises. It exists on its own merits.

The problem of holding a workpiece can be difficult, and it is, of course, dependent upon size, shape, height and weight. The usual holding tools are cramps (see Plate 13). Relief work is best held with one or more 'G' cramps, this being their shape. They come as a rule in six sizes, 3 in., 4 in., 5 in., 6 in., 8 in., and 10 in. One important thing to remember is that the holding head of the 'G' cramp must have a piece of wood placed between it and the surface which is being carved. When you turn the tightening screw you will not be conscious of the great pressure which is exerted, but this can bruise the grain, forcing it down until it becomes impacted. Hence that scrap of wood. When your chisel or gouge encounters this hard and bruised area, which may be important to the carving, you will soon realize the importance of that scrap of wood as a buffer.

For those able to afford them, carvers' chops are ideal, but in recent years the manufacturers have had difficulty in finding suitable wood from which to make them. Chops are the carving version of the vice, and they are fitted with a substantial screw thread, the jaws being faced with cork to protect the carving.

Another way of holding work is in an engineer's revolving vice, although nowadays they do not seem to make them with sufficient jaw width to accommodate large carvings. But the idea of being able to revolve work at will and to secure it instantly in any position is an attractive one.

The traditional way of holding the majority of workpieces is by means of the bench dogs, as in the Sjoberg bench. These depend on the action of a large end-vice which is built into an extending platform, the top of which is bored through at intervals of $4\frac{1}{2}$ in. with a square hole to take the dog, which is a solid piece of metal with a sprung section to take up the tightening action as the end-vice closes. The second dog is located in the static section of the bench. By a screwing action the workpiece is held tightly between the dogs (see 15A and B).

One of the oldest methods of holding a workpiece is by the use of the carver's bench screw (see Plate 16). In the modern version this is a tool with a threaded pointed shaft around which revolves a large wing nut. The shaft of the bench screw passes up through the bench (it is, of course, necessary to bore a hole through the bench or kitchen table beforehand and it should make a flush fit), and the pointed end pierces the block of wood for carving. The screw, which is underneath the bench, is then tightened to capacity. It is advisable to use a block of wood as a 'washer'. An advantage of using the bench screw is that you can move the work round from time to time. Screws are used mainly for carving in the round, because relief work is too thin to take the pointed end of the screw.

Apart from chops, dogs and bench screws for holding workpieces rigid, there are various metal clips on the market for securing relief panels. For myself, I generally allow some surplus area and use a couple of 'G' cramps. The bruised area is later sawn off.

The hard-up carver can easily improvise his own inexpensive method of holding relief work. The only snag is that it necessitates injuring the surface of the bench. It is done by plain bench stops, which are ordinary blocks of wood. Their size will vary according to the workpiece, but the main idea is to enclose the workpiece, sometimes on three sides when it has to be released and moved round, sometimes on four sides when you are able to move round the work.

This seems to be an opportune moment to explain the business of maintaining carving tools. We are concerned with one thing, how to sharpen them. Many promising carvers have lost not only their tempers but also a growing interest in carving simply because they cannot manage to put an edge on chisels, gouges and parting tools. It is no use bundling the lot up and taking them to the man who sharpens scissors for a living. He will cheerfully accept the job and charge you very little for doing it. Having paid him, you will find them all well blued, their temper gone through overheating. It is no use shoving the onus of sharpening on to the tool dealer or the do-it-yourself shop. Some will tell you that it may take weeks to get them done, others will say that it is a skilled job and they do not want the responsibility of ruining them . . .

But in a way all this frustration is a good thing, because it means that from the very start the carver must teach himself how to sharpen his own tools.

When you buy new tools they are what is known as 'factory sharpened', and they cannot be used at once, because they are blunt. They need a final edge. It does not matter how long this takes. An hour on one chisel is nothing until you get used to it. This is where you need patience to avoid later frustration.

You will require one or two inexpensive items in order to put the edge on your tools. These are investments which will yield a much better dividend than any stocks and shares.

First of all, you have a choice between a manually operated grindstone or a circular carborundum stone which can be used in conjunction with a power

A

15 *Bench dogs, which are used in pairs. When the dog is in position the wood is placed against the sprung section, then tightened up for a secure hold. In B, the dogs are shown flat against the positioning holes in the bench. Photographer: Derek Gabriel*

B

16 *Bench screw. Length $7\frac{1}{4}$ in.*

17 *Photographs A, B and C show the rolling motion to be used when sharpening the gouge. This is obtained by a smooth wrist action. In D the inside curve of the gouge is being treated by the slipstone to remove small burrs. Chisels are finished on the buff-hide strop (E), dressed with rouge or crocus powder. A one-way stroke must be used, otherwise the tool will pierce the hide.*

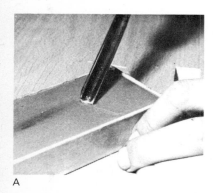

A

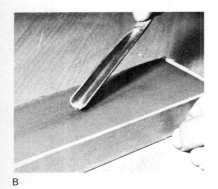

B

C

tool which is clamped in a metal stand and clamped down for stability during sharpening. It leaves both hands free to manipulate the tool, and the only objection to this is the speed, which is as a rule 900 or 2,400 r.p.m. If the tool is in contact with the grinding wheel a moment too long, it goes blue with overheating and this denotes a loss of temper. Of course, you should always damp down a grinding wheel with plenty of water, but when you do this with an unguarded power tool the water ends up on the ceiling and walls. One recent invention is a device for slowing down the speed, but this is still too fast for grinding purposes.

The wheel which I personally favour is manually operated and made especially for the job. The stone itself is blue grit bilston, 8 in., 10 in., or 12 in. in diameter with a turned spindle and iron trough in which water rests. The wheel is dampened as it revolves. The drawback with this particular model is that you cannot turn the handle and sharpen the tool at the same time, so you must have a helper to turn at the proper speed to avoid that ruinous blueing. But I am told that treadle-operated models are available, and this seems to be the answer.

When you grind a new tool for the first time you can put the edge in exactly the right position. If you fail, then re-grind it. This will mean a loss of only a fraction of the metal. But take the greatest care when sharpening gouges and parting tools. Chisels are much easier, of course, because they are either straight or oblique (known as 'corner' chisels).

As mentioned earlier, factory sharpened tools are unsuitable for immediate work because they are relatively blunt. But in addition to this they generally arrive with a bevel of approximately 25 degrees, whereas the carver requires a bevel of less than 15 degrees. The 25 degree angle is much too steep for use on detailed and intricate carving. In the case of gouges the bevel can, of course, taper off gradually in relation to the shaft. A cutting edge of 15 to 20 degrees is suitable for soft woods, but 20 to 25 degrees is best for hard woods.

Sharpening consists of a number of separate operations, including grinding, whetting, honing and stropping (see Plates 17A–F).

Having sharpened the tool on the grinding wheel, you can now make the edge really sharp. It cannot be over-emphasized that dull tools lead to frustration and a rapid disenchantment with wood carving. Instead of causing a divorce we should work hard to keep this love affair between wood and steel flourishing.

Oilstones, which can be natural or manufactured, should be part of your basic equipment, and they should be washed from time to time in petrol or boiled in a dilute solution of soda. Natural stones are slower to impart an edge, and it is a good idea to have one of each, because first stage sharpening can be done on a manufactured stone, then completed on a natural one. Carborundum stones are in two grades with a coarse surface on one side and a fine, or, alternatively, a medium one on the other. The usual size is 8 in.×2 in., but stones for finishing, known as Arkansas or Washita, are slightly smaller as a rule. I like the Arkansas stone, because it is almost pure white and it has a pleasurable bite as it meets the tool steel. Other stones are the Dalmore or Shammy, which is supplied 6 in.×2 in.×1 in., in medium and fine qualities, or in India Combination of fine and coarse. The lubricant for any stone is a fine oil, from bicycle to typewriter. Never use linseed oil on oilstones, because it only clogs up the fine pores and dulls the sharpening quality.

Of course, you should not use the oilstone without preparation. When you buy one it must be primed, and this is done by soaking it thoroughly in oil and kerosene in a ratio of two parts of oil to one of kerosene. Continue the soaking for three or four days, and turn it daily, because this will provide a good working surface and discourage steel fragments from working into the pores.

When you sharpen a curved tool on a stone, keep rolling it from left to right to ensure an even pressure on each of the planes. This takes some practice, but if you adopt a wrist movement and hold the tool at the correct angle, you will soon become skilled.

After you have used the stone, you should trim the edge of the tool to free any fine burrs, and this is done with the slipstone, which is supplied in a series of shapes to match the various contours of the tools, from kidney shaped to triangular wedge. Slip stones are made from the same materials as oil stones, and should be as well lubricated. When you use one, hold it in the hand and work it against the tool.

Lastly, you will require a strop. This is made from buff hide, 2½ in. × 7 in. or 3 in. × 10 in., and dressed with crocus powder, Carborundum No. 400 grit or just plain spit, which is as good as anything. Another lubricant is emery paste, but it should be used sparingly. It is a good idea to cut off a small piece of the strop for use on the inner side of veiners, fluters and gouges. The strop should be securely fastened to a block of wood about 2 in. thick with impact adhesive or screws, which are driven well below the surface to avoid chipping your tools against the heads. The strop should be kept supple with light oil.

When the tools are in use during carving, the bench should be kept as tidy as possible. This is more difficult than it sounds. Some carvers use a kind of box with a slotted vertical rest built into it to hold tools not in use, others talk their wives into making a strong canvas holdall with tool loops sewn into it. Whatever the method adopted, the important thing is to avoid merely chucking the tools down when they have done their stint, because this only blunts the edges, and you end up making more sharpening work for yourself. Although tools are made of steel and steel is hard, the fine edges can nick very easily.

Some non-carving handymen think that carving tools are rather quaint implements with a million and one uses, and they can be quite merciless in their borrowings. If you have not yet mustered enough nerve to turn the borrowers down pointblank, just suggest that you treat them to a set. Even if they do take you up on it, the price will be incredibly cheap compared with the replacement of borrowed, lost or damaged carving tools.

Of course, the problem of personal tools can be very difficult in schools, and boys are inveterate borrowers. This can actually be turned astutely to an educational advantage if you let borrowers know that they must resharpen the tools before returning them. Ideally, of course, there should be as many complete sets as there are members of the class.

Teachers and beginners of all ages will very soon become aware of the need for certain safety measures when using edged tools. Men should never wear ties while working. In any case, whoever heard of a craftsman wearing such a thing? Carving can be warm work, and the more bodily ventilation you have, the better. It also happens to be pretty dry work, and a mug of tea, cider or plain water will keep you articulate when you are in conversation with onlookers, who tend to say things like: 'And you're carving that – ah – that thing out of a single block of wood, are you? Well, I never . . .'

The initiation into carving is often bloody, made so by the majority of beginners forgetting the cardinal rule: *never cut towards your body, hand or arm*! A misjudged blow with the mallet and chisel or gouge can whip straight through the wood and into your hand. Sometimes it also removes a fragment of your finger. Once, when carving in a bad light, I ran a gouge

17F *The honing gauge has a limited use when sharpening wood carving chisels, because it does not provide the acute angle required. But for general utility chisels it is recommended, because it provides a uniform angle. The final honing is shown here.*

D

E

F

along my finger, taking a surgically clean-cut piece with it. Carefully putting the carving aside so that it would not become gory and interfere with the final finish, I tried holding the finger under a tap. This failed, so I tried binding it up. Four or five handkerchiefs later I started off along the road to the local hospital. The Casualty sister naturally wanted to know how it had happened. I explained that I was carving wood. She glanced at the clock. 'At three in the morning?' Well, that's how carving takes you. But there is a moral and it is, always keep a well-stocked first-aid box handy, especially in schools.

If you have good sharp tools, then accidents should happen very seldom, because you can gauge their action. Blunt tools which have to be bullied or bulldozed through the wood will become wilful and may turn round and bite you.

The other requirement is good lighting. Granted, not all of us can have our benches and kitchen tables under windows, but modern lighting is so well developed that there is no excuse for working in semi-darkness and gloom. I use a fairly powerful top lighting, and occasionally employ a small desk lamp, too (see Plate 18), especially when carving reliefs. This has an additional advantage, because relief work depends for much of its effect upon lighting, and the manipulation of a desk lamp during the carving helps you to judge the future play of light on the work.

A

19 *In 'A' a flexidrive is being used and the advantage is ease of manipulation.*
In 'B' the burr is in the chuck of the tool, and more muscle is needed for complete control.

B

48

Fussy amateurs often wear long white aprons, which makes them look like surgeons performing brain operations. Unless you wish to give the same impression, stick to your usual leisure attire. You will soon get used to chips and shavings working their way down your shirt front and into your waistband, and your hair will quickly take on a slightly distinguished appearance from the dusting of sawdust. It is probably better to disrobe in your workshop and shed all this stuff in situ before you go to bed. Wood carvers are sufficiently unorthodox not to mind passing through the house in the nude.

Reference has already been made to the use of power tools for wood carving (see Plates 19A and B). The peculiar thing about power tools is that they have their own influence on the wood. It is inconceivable that you could create even a reasonable facsimile of a hand carving with a power tool.

If you run a power tool for a long period – say more than twenty minutes at a time – it will overheat. If you hold one hand on the casing while the motor is running, the metal will be warm. After high speed operation it will get hot, and this is the signal to switch off and cool it. The speed of motors varies from model to model, but the usual range is from 500 to 2,800 r.p.m.

Sanding, which can speed up the preparation of wood for carving or for the finishing, is done by a disc attachment to the power tool or by the use of an orbital sander. The disc is flexible or on a ball joint, and it needs a smooth and even pressure. Orbital sanders have a rectangular pad which moves back and forth in a $\frac{3}{16}$ in. orbit about 4,600 times per minute. The advantage of the orbital sander is that the circular sanding marks are practically invisible.

One other sander should be mentioned, and this is the drum, or spindle, sander which is sold as a rule in sets of five with diameters from $\frac{1}{2}$ in. to 2 in. The only thing against the drum sander is the amount of kick back, which can damage a carving, especially when you are smoothing an edge or an inside contour.

It is possible to carve in two ways with a power tool. You can hold the tool itself to the work or you can employ a flexidrive. The only thing against the use of the power tool is the weight, which can be considerable if work continues for long periods. Perhaps the flexidrive is the real answer to this. The ideal length is 40 in., and it has a $\frac{1}{4}$ in. diameter spindle for engagement with the power drill chuck. At the other end is a $\frac{3}{8}$ in. diameter chuck fitted with a key. The flexidrive accepts twist drills, rotary burrs and mounted points in addition to polishing mops which can be used for finishing.

Power tool carving makes use of drills but mostly burrs made of hardened steel with $\frac{1}{4}$ in. diameter shanks. For a time the beginner may have difficulty in controlling the action, because they wedge, chatter or bounce, but this can be corrected by a firm pressure. They should be moved from right to left for a hard bite on the wood and the quick removal of the wood, and left to right for smooth finishing or the fining down of delicate edges.

And now a word about your health. Whenever possible, sit down to do your carving. Make yourself a stool of the right height for the bench. Standing up for hours on end may give you that obscure complaint, Carver's Ankle, which no doctor has so far been able to cure.

Lastly, do not work for more than twenty-four hours at a stretch on a particularly engrossing carving. Carvers should keep their strength up and eat heartily.

And when you reach the stage when people start offering you money for your simplest carvings, you can consider leaving that boring bread-and-butter job to become a full-time professional carver.

4

Woods

Wood and timber do not amount to quite the same thing in the trade. If we are to be strictly accurate wood is the substance which is found in the veins of leaves and in shrub twigs. Timber, on the other hand, means wood produced by trees over a certain size. The trees capable of producing timber can be broken down into two classes, conifers and dicotyledons or deciduous trees. The conifers are represented by pines, spruces and larches with the seeds contained in cones and having 'needle' leaves. Among the deciduous trees are teak, oak, beech and ash with large flat leaves and seeds enclosed in seed cases. They are the hardwoods.

A tree grows at the ends of its branches for length, but as far as girth is concerned in trunks and branches, new wood and bark is created by a layer of cells situated between wood and bark. This is a kind of thrusting outwards of the cells, and it leads to an increase in girth of the tree. In the temperate zones new wood grows throughout the spring and part of the summer, going into suspended animation for the autumn and winter. The reason for the rings, which can be seen in a crosscut section, is that early wood is quite different from the wood which grows later in the year. The two types are known as springwood and summerwood (or autumnwood).

Softwood consists of spindle-shaped fibres (*tracheids*) which are parallel to the trunk axis. Some, such as pines, also have resin ducts. At right angles to the fibres run certain thin-looking structures, located between the outside of the trunk and the pith, and they contain sugar, starch or fatty oil and albuminous substances.

After a tree is felled and the cells start dying, the sapwood undergoes a change and becomes heartwood, and an infiltration of tannins, gums and resins takes place. This is followed by the gradual shrinkage of the structure.

Timberyard workers often talk about wood being 'wet' before it is dried and seasoned, but this does not mean that it is absolutely saturated. Water content is a percentage of the weight of the wood. A log of wood contains about 200 lb of water to every 100 lb of dry wood.

All this has a bearing on carving woods, but the Wood Comparison Tables, which follow, are not intended as inflexible guides. There is very little point in being dogmatic about which woods to choose and which to avoid, because some woods suit some carvers and other woods are preferred by others. So it is impossible to be specific about any particular wood and its predictable behaviour unless we know beforehand exactly what it is going to be used for. Although an experienced carver may dislike working in oak, for instance, it is quite common to find a youngster who can work miracles with it. Because opinions of wood and the abilities of carvers vary greatly, the wise teacher will take care not to thrust preconceived and theoretical notions about the qualities of various woods down the throats of pupils. Most of the opinions which we hold about wood can never be anything more than comparative. The learner must be permitted to explore wood, all kinds of wood, including hard, soft, close and open grained, working in large and small pieces.

Anybody with an eye for pattern must come very quickly to appreciate the figuring of wood, which is caused by the way the grain is formed. The lace-like, whorled or straight figuring will come to play a definite role in the carving. This represents the real prelude to the marriage between wood and design, and in this sense many carvings will begin not so much as preconceptions as an exploration of what the wood itself is willing to do. A great deal of abstract work will involve 'doodling' with gouge and chisel, and it becomes a kind of wandering about until the wood itself will suddenly take over and tell you what to do with it. This does not apply to all carving, of course, but for the teacher it is useful when pupils reach the stage of finding out for themselves how to create design.

Early in the business of becoming a carver you will have to learn how to select wood. When you boil it down, all it really means is knowing the raw material which is best suited to your particular project. At best, this is still a rather hit and miss affair, because not every piece of wood can be X-rayed, and no timberyard manager will go to the length of guaranteeing that the piece you purchase will be absolutely free of flaws and knots. The best that can be said of the wide variety of wood available is that each one possesses a certain set of characteristics, the combination of which makes it suitable, not quite suitable or completely unsuitable for carving. It has been impossible to include every single known wood in the Tables at the end of this section, because a full world list would fill several volumes about twice the size of this one. Another reason for omission is that many woods look deceptive in terms of digital assessment. Lime, for instance, is one of the carver's favourites, much used for figure work from the earliest times. It is a delight to work with and it finishes beautifully, but it would be almost impossible to sum up its pleasures in four or five digital ratings. It simply does not 'datarise'. But where digital comparison is useful in deciding whether a particular job will match a certain wood, we can use the Tables, and this applies, for instance, to pine. The characteristics of six species will be found in the Tables, and on the basis of digital assessment the White Northern Pine is the best choice. It is readily obtainable from most timberyards. The next best is the Limber Pine.

As rule-of-thumb stuff, it is easy enough to know which wood to choose for large and small carvings. A large and simple-lined carving is best done in a wood with an open grain – chestnut, mahogany, basswood, walnut or oak, for instance. These are all woods which withstand bold cutting and will accept a certain amount of detail. Small carvings, on the other hand, are best done in the close-grained woods, such as lime, apple, box or ebony, and most of them carve like cheese.

General rules about wood selection are simple to remember. The wood must be sound and free from splits. But when you see wood stacked in a timberyard you will often notice many splits in the sawn ends. This does not necessarily mean that the wood is split along the entire length, because the middle section or the far end may be quite sound. If the wood you happen to fancy is situated in the middle of a tall stack, it is unlikely that the foreman will have the entire stack moved on the off-chance of pleasing you, especially if you require only a foot or two. In fairness to timberyard people, they will not deliberately let you take bad wood away with you, but if you really want a piece from the middle of a stack you may be asked to wait for a week or two, when they have time to do the job. In the educational field, schools are quite safe in ordering miscellaneous lots of blocks, planks and offcuts for teaching purposes, and the selection can be left to the timberyard foreman.

Although I have harped on about the importance of sound wood there may be times when it does not apply, because some carvers will deliberately select a piece of wood which contains knots and burls destined to play their own part in the future carving. A burl, by the way, is a malformation of the tree structure during growth, and it creates a swirled effect, often of great beauty.

Another thing to consider when selecting wood is the grain. Some carvings are done across the grain, others are cut with, or along, the grain. For teaching purposes it is best to use wood with the grain running along it, because it is much easier to work. For cross-grain working you need really sharp tools.

One test of good sound wood is to give it a solid thwack with a mallet, taking care not to bruise it. It should ring out audibly, whereas wood which lets out a dull and soggy thud should not be bought, because it will probably have a high moisture content or a lot of structural flaws.

Timberyard men use a common parlance when describing the way wood is sawn. *Quarter sawn* means that the wood is cut so that the annual rings are at 45 degrees, and it applies to hard woods. Where soft woods are concerned, sawing is described as *edge grained*.

When you finally decide on a piece it should be planed before you take it away, and a small fee is charged for putting it through the machine. But do not ask the yard men to sand the wood down, because this causes grit and silica dust to lodge in the grain, and it could damage your tools when you start carving.

Before we consider in detail some of the main woods and their properties, a word to teachers of carving in schools and other institutions. It is a good idea – and probably an essential one – to assemble as many different specimens as possible, both planed and unplaned, some with the bark on, and cut in such a way as to show the figuring. Some sides should be finished, some left in a natural state for comparison purposes. The blocks should be cut to a shape which makes them convenient for handling and inspection by pupils, and a recommended size is 9½ in. × 3½ in. × 1 in. thick. Each block should be labelled on one side with the common and botanical names, the area of the world where the tree grows, and the approximate age of this particular piece. Age is, of course, assessed by using a magnifying glass to count the rings. It is a good idea to turn the blocks over after inspection so that the labels are face downwards. The pupils should then attempt to identify each block by appearance alone, recounting some of the facts about it. It should be possible for teachers of carving to arrange for the botany teacher to give one or two lessons on the growth and ecology of trees and the economics of forestry, thereby linking an ancient craft with Natural History and the financial contribution which trees make to the economy. Senior pupils should be taken on field trips to see trees *in situ*.

Here are some practical and useful observations on various common carving woods . . .

Basswood is good for carving when your tools are in first class condition. Some interesting colours will emerge, and it takes practically any finish.

Cypress is a fairly soft wood, but it does not take a finish very well.

Cedar is good for chip carving, but it is seldom available in large pieces.

Beech is a good wood for light, or shallow, relief carving, but it is not too dependable when it comes to deeper cut work.

Oak varies, but in general it is reliable for all types of carving. In colour it runs through a wide spectrum from white to red. Red oak tends to splinter, and white oak is the best choice.

Mahogany is very even-grained, red to brown, and excellent for carving purposes. It comes from several different countries, including Africa, Spain, America, the West Indies and Mexico, and varies from one area to another.

Walnut is close grained and difficult to carve as a rule. It is not generally available in timberyards.

Cherry is a good carving wood for fine detail.

Rosewood is noted for its colouring, which runs from red to purple, but it is not particularly easy to carve, due to its hardness.

Holly is chalk to yellow in colour and is fairly easy to work.

Birch is good wood for teaching purposes, and the natural brown colour is enhanced by the proper finishing.

Plane has many of the characteristics of birch, though with better figuring.

Teak is useful for the advanced carver. It is strong, it carves well and has a characteristic brown hue.

Obeche is not simple or easy to carve due to its softness, but the light yellow colour is attractive.

Pear is like carving cheese, and there is an almost total absence of grain. It is good for the most intricate detail.

The reader will now appreciate the fact that any old piece of wood will not do for carving. Most of us spend months looking for a particular piece for a project. During the hunt we often find other pieces which may come in handy for other things. I once needed a piece of best oak, and during the search my wife noticed a piece of blackened railway post lying in the long grass on the banks of the Menai Straits in North Wales. It proved to be a piece of prime pine with interesting striped figuring, caused by prolonged soaking with creosote, but it turned out to be better than any wood I could buy in a timberyard.

A lot of wood comes to you by accident – that is, unless you are in the fortunate position of being able to buy any wood you need from a timberyard or one of the specialist dealers who can supply exotic woods to carvers. My own development was conditioned by one mundane factor, hard cash. I bought the best tools and, as soon as I had enough money, I bought lengths of pine planking, six to ten feet long and up to two inches thick. This was the material for my first experiments in wall decorations, reliefs and some small dimensional carvings.

Of course, when you buy wood you have to know something about it. Newly cut wood is moist and full of water. As the wood dries out, it shrinks, and if this happens too quickly, the wood splits. Sometimes these splits close up again of their own accord, although it may take months and you cannot count on it happening every time, because a lot depends on the surrounding temperature. If splitting does occur and closure of the splits seems slow, some plastic wood can be used as a filler. Bear in mind that plastic wood is subject to shrinkage as it dries out, and it is therefore a good idea to over-fill the cracks, then any excess can be cut away with a chisel, or sandpapered down when it sets hard.

Much of the wood which reaches the timberyard is only partly dried out, and final seasoning is carried out under controlled conditions, sometimes by natural air drying, sometimes in the kilns. Most drying is done by kilning for economic reasons, because air drying takes a long time – a 2 in. thick plank can occupy up to six months, often longer. Not all woods can be kilned, however, and many exotic woods would be ruined by such treatment, so the merchant stacks them in open-walled sheds. The process can take between two and four years and this, plus general overheads and shipping costs, explains why rare woods are expensive. But to the carver no fine wood is really expensive.

When you visit a timberyard, ask to see the kilns. The pipes which carry and radiate heat run all the way up to the ceiling, and a series of jets inject steam to create a controlled humidity. The timber is stacked in such a way as to permit the atmosphere to reach every part of the wood, and most kilns are fitted with fans to move the air round the wood.

Despite the high degree of wood technology which has been reached, kilning still encounters the traditional difficulties, and it is interesting to hear what a craftsman of the 'eighties, George Sturt, had to say about work in his day. 'No care on earth could prevent the elm from drying "curly" as we said, that is to say with a sort of ripple in the grain, making narrow and shallow cross waves from one end of the board to the other . . . The elm boards insisted on going curly; the oak and ash planks stubbornly bent all along the centre into a kind of shallow trough on the one side with corresponding lumpiness on the other. The better the timber the likelier it was to develop these defects in seasoning.'*

You will find timberyard people very obliging. I went to my own supplier recently and asked for a 12 in.×12 in.×12 in. block of sycamore. It was a difficult order. My idea was to carve four primitive faces, one on each side of this giant cube. It necessitated a special order, but the piece was cut from the middle of a prime log and ready for collection within a week.

Not all wood comes from timberyards or is found by accident. If you want mahogany or oak and you cannot afford timberyard prices, the other source is the auction room, where large pieces of often ugly and unwanted furniture come under the hammer every week. Much heavy and dated

20 'Man-Made, Nature-Made' by the author. An abstract carving, or wood sculpture, like this one, evolves or grows. It can be viewed from several different angles, and provides a variety of impressions. The sides are contoured in bold sweeps. Lime and mahogany. 9 in.×3¾ in. Clear polished. Photograph by Derek Gabriel. See also page 64.

* George Sturt: *The Wheelwright's Shop*. Cambridge University Press. 1963.

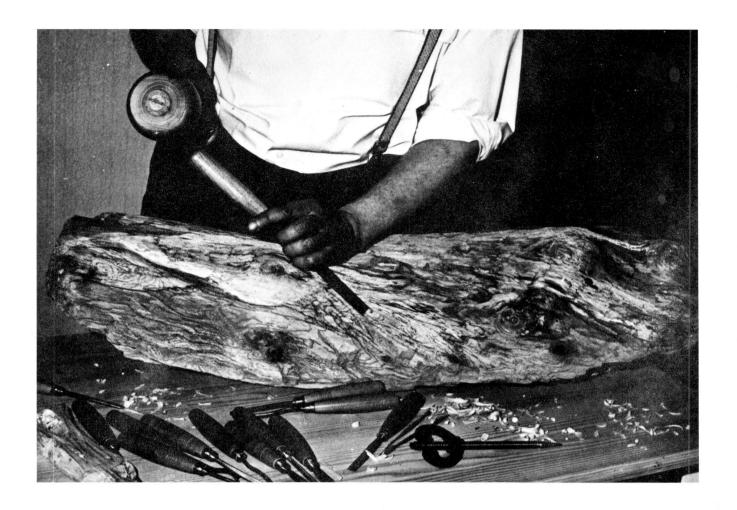

21 *This log, found on the shores of the Bristol Channel, took six months to dry out and a further ten days to rough trim. In this picture I am just starting work on it with the intention of carving the wings of three sea birds. Mahogany. 33 in. long. Photograph by Derek Gabriel.*

furniture will yield three or four pieces of solid oak or mahogany. While you may have to bleach out up to fifty to seventy years of various wax polishes, varnishes and shellac, and possibly sandpaper away a lot of the underlayer, where the wood has soaked up seeping polishes, then press on to cut away the elaborately turned curves and faces, the result can be worthwhile. When I finally reach the wood itself, I plunge it into the bath for a scrub with a dilute bleach to get rid of any last traces of old polish. You can expect a great deal of wastage when you buy old furniture, and you should watch out for worm-holes, but you can still count yourself fortunate in acquiring some of the finest cabinet wood used at a time when furniture was made solidly, not out of plywood, chipboard and veneer, and steamed into position.

As you go on carving through a lifetime you are bound to acquire different pieces of wood in various shapes and sizes, and mark them down for future use. One carver I know likes to have his 'stock' scattered around his workroom so that he can study shapes, colours and absorb the appearance of the wood. This sort of thing is a good stimulus for creative thought, and it is something which the teacher should do rather than having everything stacked neatly away, where the students cannot see it until it is brought out for use.

As I write I realize that I have a 10 ft × 8 in. × 2 in. thick piece of 200-year-old English oak in the hall, a fine piece of elm intended for a carved table, two 6 ft lengths of Parana and Columbian pine, and several pieces of good furniture mahogany stored in the main passageways of my home. True, they may not be very ornamental, but it means about five years of carving in waiting. In a strained and tense world this is a comfort. Elsewhere, many blocks of machined lime rest amongst my books, and when I move from the desk a driftwood log, cast up by the Bristol Channel tides, trips me (see Plate 21). My mind keeps wandering to half a tree, embedded like part of a petrified dinosaur, in the soft sands of Llangennith, and I am frustrated to realize that it is too heavy to move.

Driftwood has its own magic, and it automatically creates speculation. My wife and I gather lots of pieces on the beaches of the Gower Peninsula in South Wales. The action of sea and sand imparts a silky feeling to it, and it takes on shapes, it 'speaks', and sometimes the imaginative carver can marry it to something else (see Plate 20, 'Man-Made, Nature-Made). The chief virtue of driftwood is shape, and for this reason it is not generally a good idea to mess it up with too much elaborate carving, because the shape has already been made by that master carver, the sea.

If you want to carve driftwood, then it must first be treated to a good wash to get rid of all that clinging sand, which can damage your tools. It is best to use slightly tepid water to dissolve the salt crystals, and a soft nail brush should be used to get into the cracks where sand particles lodge.

If the fibres of the wood are soaked by the sea, then let the wood dry out slowly in a normal room temperature. It is as a rule already well seasoned, and so there is little damage by cracking or splitting. Drying time is governed by bulk. One of my logs took more than six months to dry out, losing more than one third of its weight in the process and turning a grey-silver.

A COMPARISON TABLE OF FIFTY WOODS

Weight: approximately lb per cubic foot of wood.
Shrinkage: comparative figures (related to a maximum of 200).
Hardness: comparative figures (related to a maximum of 100).

Name of Wood	Weight	Shrinkage	Hardness	Workability	Remarks
Alder, Red	28	123	50	Good	Pink to brown in colour
Ash, Black	34	150	64	Good	Dark brown
Ash, Green	40	122	70	Good	Goes brown on exposure to air
Ash, White	41	126	75	Good	Brown to red
Basswood	26	160	31	Good	Cream coloured with close grain
Beech	45	162	96	Variable	Close grain
Birch, Grey	35	147	54	Fair	Close grain
Birch, Yellow	43	166	86	Fair	Close grain
Cedar, Alaska	31	91	53	Good	Close grain
Cedar, Red	33	78	81	Good	Close grain
Cedar, White Northern	22	69	30	Good	Close grain
Cherry, Black	35	113	72	Difficult	Close grain
Chestnut	30	111	50	Good	Grey to brown
Cypress	32	104	52	Fair	Close grain

Name of Wood	Weight	Shrinkage	Hardness	Workability	Remarks
Douglas Fir	30	103	52	Good	Yellow
Elder, Box	36	149	68	Good	Close grain
Elm	36	145	66	Variable	Light brown. Close grain
Eucalyptus, Australian	49	—	95	Difficult	Brittle
Fir, Alpine	26	103	31	Good	White or nearly white
Fir, Red	27	114	52	Variable	
Fir, White	26	95	42	Fair	White with hint of pink to red
Gum, Red	34	150	60	Fair	Red to brown
Hemlock, Western	29	120	50	Fair	White to cream
Hickory	53	182	17	Difficult	Red-brown
Holly	40	155	86	Variable	Close grain
Ironwood	80	125	100	Difficult	Close grain
Larch, Western	36	129	64	Fair	Red-brown
Lignum Vitae	80	Minimal	100	Difficult	Very close grain
Mahogany, W. African	42	nil	75	Difficult	Dark brown to red
Mahogany, W. Indian	34	nil	60	Difficult	Dark brown to red
Maple, Black	40	140	97	Fair	Red to brown
Maple, Red	38	128	79	Fair	Red to brown. Close grain
Maple, Silver	33	114	65	Fair	Red to brown. Close grain
Maple, Striped	32	121	59	Fair	Close grain
Oak, Black	60	142	100	Difficult	Close grain
Pine, Jack	30	102	48	Good	Light colour
Pine, Limber	28	80	39	Good	Light colour
Pine, Loblolly	38	127	62	Good	Light colour
Pine, Norway	34	116	46	Good	Orange to red and brown
Pine, Pitch	34	110	56	Good	Resinous
Pine, White Northern	25	83	35	Good	Close grain
Poplar, Yellow	28	119	40	Fair	Close grain
Redwood	30	65	59	Fair	Deep red to brown
Spruce, Black	28	112	40	Fair	Resinous and close grain
Spruce, Red	28	117	41	Fair	Resinous and close grain
Spruce, White	28	134	37	Fair	Resinous and close grain
Sycamore	35	136	64	Difficult	Close grain and light coloured
Walnut, Black	39	116	88	Fair	Dark brown
Willow, Black	26	126	35	Fair	Dark brown
Yew	44	128	53	Difficult	Dark brown

TABLE OF GRAINS OF SIXTY-FIVE WOODS

Name of Wood	Silky	Fine	Close	Straight	Coarse	Interlocked	Figured	Hard	Soft
Abura		★		★		★		★	
Afara			★	★				★	
Agba		★		★				★	
Alder			★	★				★	
Ash				★	★			★	
Beech		★	★	★			★	★	
Birch		★	★	★				★	
Blackbean				★	★	★		★	
Cedar, Europe			★	★				★	
Cedar, Canadian	★			★			★		★
Chestnut			★		★	★		★	
Cypress		★		★					★
Ebony			★	★				★	
Elm					★		★	★	
Fir	★	★	★						★
Gaboon				★		★		★	
Greenheart		★		★		★		★	
Guarea		★		★				★	
Gurjun					★	★		★	
Haldu		★		★		★		★	
Hemlock				★			★		★
Hornbeam		★		★				★	
Idigbo	★				★	★		★	
Iroko					★	★	★	★	
Jariah				★	★	★		★	
Larch		★		★					★
Laurel		★		★				★	
Lime	★	★	★	★				★	
Mahogany, African				★	★	★		★	
Mahogany, C. American				★	★	★	★	★	
Mahogany, S. American	★	★	★				★	★	
Mandio					★			★	
Maple			★					★	

Name of Wood	Silky	Fine	Close	Straight	Coarse	Interlocked	Figured	Hard	Soft
Meranti			★				★	★	
Oak, European				★	★		★	★	
Oak, Japanese				★				★	
Oak, Silky	★				★			★	
Oak, Tasmanian				★	★		★	★	
Obeche		★		★		★	★		★
Padouk					★	★	★	★	
Pear		★					★	★	
Peroba, Red		★	★	★				★	
Pillarwood		★		★				★	
Pine, Parana		★	★	★					★
Pine, Pitch		★	★	★					★
Pine, White				★	★				★
Pine, Yellow				★					★
Plane		★		★				★	
Podo		★					★		★
Poplar		★		★				★	
Ramin		★		★		★		★	
Rauli	★	★	★	★				★	
Redwood			★						★
Rosewood, S. American			★	★				★	
Rosewood, Indian			★	★	★	★		★	
Sapele				★	★			★	
Satinwood	★	★	★	★		★	★	★	
Spruce, Canadian		★		★					★
Spruce, European	★			★					★
Sycamore	★	★	★	★			★	★	
Teak				★	★		★	★	
Walnut, Black American		★		★			★	★	
Walnut, European	★	★	★				★	★	
Willow		★		★				★	
Yew		★	★	★			★		★

5

Simplicity is not an aim in art.
You come to it in spite of
yourself.

Brancusi

Traditional and Contemporary Design

It is hardly sufficient to be adept in the use of tools. You must also create. The basis of creation is design, whether from nature or from the mind.

Some people complain that they feel lost for 'things to carve'. They simply do not know where to find ideas. This is an absurd complaint, but it adds yet another reason why wood carving should be taught as a separate subject, and not crammed into 'woodwork' or 'handicrafts'. If the carver is to be creative, then he must be persuaded to adventure widely not only in the exploration of shape and form but in other more material fields. The cultures of the world provide an enormous reservoir.

A carver needs two skills, the skill with tools and the skill with form. A slavish copying of natural forms is itself anachronistic, because unless you are a Grinling Gibbons you cannot render in wood the exact form of a leaf or a bird or a horse any more than you can paint photographically. Such copying is pointless except for practice purposes and experience in the use of the tools. In the end interpretation and the many personal nuances which make us people, each in our own right, creep into it. On this basis wood carving is just as creative as other forms of art.

60

Because the tools of carving have changed so little since they were evolved hundreds and thousands of years ago, we still use the same practical techniques as the early carvers. The essential and significant difference is that we do not *think* as did our forerunners. In simple terms this explains the evolution of design in carving. To understand the meaning of design we have to remember that commercial carvers and creative carvers are birds of two different feathers in the twentieth century. The commercial carver is at a disadvantage, because he is as a rule in the hands of his client as far as design is concerned, and clients are notoriously conservative. The only originality worth the name springs from independent carvers who work to please themselves and from teachers who have sufficient freedom to experiment. The Who's Who at the end of this book lists some of them.

Another contrast between carvers of past and present should be remembered. In medieval times the carving was done by people who were considered to be artists in their own right, and so the master carver and his apprentices worked in an atmosphere of creative freedom. Today the private client is often fussy, and even that liberal sponsor, Industry, will hover nervously when a commission is handed out in case the results are so abstract as to be incomprehensible or – worse! – grossly indecent. In the sister art of stone carving, the sculptor and wood engraver, Eric Gill, was often accused of pictorial pornography. But in the richer days of the medieval carver even the element of erotic fancy and Rabelaisian whimsy was given full play in the decoration of cathedrals, churches and the great houses of the wealthy. Today we are unenlightened to the extent that many of us fail to recognize that this is work which cannot be done by more than one man, the carver himself. The old truth that a committee never composed a symphony or painted a picture holds true in carving. Any carver worth his salt works only to satisfy himself. It is interesting to note that the cottage furniture made by the poor of the seventeenth and eighteenth centuries in rural England in imitation of the furnishings of their richer masters is anaemic and clumsy stuff, lacking any distinctive style.

Yet there is no need for mental vacuity in a world so crammed with design ideas. In the present section I have tried to throw in many ideas taken from contrasting sources, but none of them should be followed to the letter, because all they represent is a series of springboards and starting points. The only originality worth the name comes from carvers who work to please themselves, not to make precise facsimiles. The illustrations which follow suggest that they are capable of transition to wood. Granted, wood is not as flexible as oil paint, pastel or pencil, textiles or clay, yet there is a very simple bridge to cross to achieve this transition, and it is a bridge which every carver will find for himself. My main intention here is to encourage self-expression and, above all, individuality.

There are still teachers who insist on their pupils carving 'pretty' little toy-like animals, profiles of Red Indian faces, birds or other things from stock designs which are diluted by one class after another until they finally lose all spirit and verve. This is the easy way out, and apart from giving the young carver confidence in the use of the tools it does nothing for his aesthetic development, which is equally important. Unless a design pushes back a fold in the mental curtain and succeeds in intriguing or exciting the beginner, there is no point in going on with it. If it is a chore even to think about the question of design, this is an indication of a wrong approach. It is here that the individual carver – oh, happy fellow! – has a great advantage. He, at least, explores and evolves a design simply because he wants to do it, as distinct from the young person who has a project thrust upon him by a

61

teacher who thinks that 'it might be a good one to try out'. What it really boils down to is the enthusiasm which the teacher should be able to communicate. If a teacher is able to let the young carver discover his own mental springboard and then leap from it to create something as personal as thought itself, then far better progress will be made and some mutual satisfaction obtained.

The future of carving design rests equally between art schools and a number of part-time carvers who are scattered throughout the world in many different countries. In the art schools carving appears to be schismatic, divided equally between the many excellent furniture departments, where carving is regarded as a means of embellishing the furniture, and the sculpture classes, where thought and experiment are freer. On balance, I believe that two separate streams of advancement are possible, one from each department, but from the standpoint of artistic development carving 'in the round' represents the individual. But here again, wood sculpture is a hybrid at a time when many sculptors lump it in with miscellaneous experiments with iron, steel, polystyrene, ciment fondu and other new and exciting materials.

The part-time carvers form a distinctive section of the carving craft, although they do not fall into definite schools, as in painting. Organization is anathema to many of them, but a great body of their work is excellent and beyond even so-called professionalism. As 'enthusiastic amateurs' – a dreadful description! – they work at their leisure, moving with purpose towards perfection. They are in the ideal situation of working alone with the privilege of making their own mistakes. The results are seldom for sale, nor are they seen in exhibitions. Hidden away throughout the world there must be many fine examples of carving, the fruits of those enthusiastic amateurs. Many of them would show an imaginative exploration of the nature of design.

Sources of design are everywhere in great variety, but my own preference for a starting point has always been anthropology. This is not to infer that you should copy the culture of other races, cut for cut. I have already used the word *springboard* several times, and anthropology provides not only springboards galore but also the means of studying architecture, weaving and pottery motifs and magic itself. One example is Celtic art, others include Columbian and Maya designs, all of which should excite any carver who is looking for something different in design and form.

The best example of the springboard principle is a personal one. The evolution of the Eskimo mask described in Section One was my own exploration. It began seven years ago. It continues.

The evolution of this particular mask has been shown at some length because it was originally a springboard idea. The carver who adopts it should not follow my own development. It is always easy enough to copy. It is much harder to think and convert the thought into reality.

Talking of copying, this can still be useful for some design purposes, because even the most slavish copier has had the experience of the work running away with him. Opposite you will see a small plaque, 'Warrior'. This was done as a result of looking at a ceremonial *hacha*, or axe, of the Mexican Vera Cruz culture. The heavy symbolism carved into the original basalt was discarded and I used only the profile, later adding the dragonfly and placing it in relation to a large knot in the wood, which I accentuated by cutting down. The original was not particularly well imbued with character or personality, but in my version the face took on a cruel and savage look, yet it also acquired personality. Some people like it, others say that it epitomizes cruelty. All told, the work occupied about nine hours in two sessions, and I applied only sufficient wood stain to mark the ridges of the wood, especially round the knot.

62

22 'Warrior' by the author. Pine.
12 in.×5½ in. *Stained and waxed.*
Photograph by Derek Gabriel

One example of an interpretation, 'Medieval Decoration', was the carving shown on Plate 23. It was done for two reasons. I had been interested in brass rubbings for a long time, and I also wanted to carve a rubbing. I also happened to have some scrap pine planking, salvaged when my wife and I were forcibly modifying a Bangor, North Wales, bookshop. I hate burning wood, so this piece stuck around, awaiting its chance in the queue of oak, mahogany and lime.

I did not copy any particular brass rubbing, but roughed one out direct on to the sandpapered wood. The whole thing occupied only one evening and part of the following morning. I am still exploring the theme, because it seems to me that brass rubbings could look very attractive as relief panels in a light coloured wood. The best finish for them is a matt. Of course, you could also 'age' them for atmosphere (*see* Section Ten: Finishing).

Ceremonial robes, vestments and trappings are traditional carving subjects, and I was attracted by the horse's head on page 65, titled 'Jousting Horse'. It was suggested by the gold and scarlet cloth caparison which adorned mounts at medieval tournaments and jousting in England. When you examine the illustration the head of the horse may not be immediately apparent. This is because I was interested primarily in the geometrical arrangement of cloth on the face of the beast. The original 'springboard' was a decorative capital in an illuminated manuscript.

From these notes the reader will appreciate how wide the catchment area for ideas can be. I do a lot of reading, but I also do a lot of looking. In my own experience ideas for carving are acquired on a highly selective basis. Some ideas are immediate, others take time to come to the surface. You also begin to know instinctively how much will be gained or lost when you put a design through the physical transition from its native material and period and into wood. Very often fussy ornamentation can be disregarded and the wood itself used for the sake of colouring and figuring. Carrying this to an extreme abstract degree, the carving on page 54 was christened 'Man-Made, Nature-Made'. It did literally carve itself, for the smooth, well-rounded and tapered piece of oak was picked up by my wife, Rhian, on the shores of the Gower Peninsula in South Wales. It was perfectly smooth and it had obviously spent months in the sea. I slipped it in my pocket and from time to time looked at it, seeing in the shape the head of an ancient seal. Although it was very tempting to carve and 'improve' it, I decided to leave it alone, and it was eventually mounted with adhesive on a piece of lime. But before doing this, I carved the lime into a rough suggestion of a human footprint to suggest how the driftwood was discovered. A slight polish finished it off. While abstract in conception, it makes different people see different things in its shape and contours. The lesson learned from doing this one is that sometimes you need do little to enhance wood. The skill is in knowing what *not* to do.

Speaking of abstracts, this is one field which new carvers should explore more than they do, for there is encouragement from the colour and figuring of wood, especially in the boles of trees, which are often discarded by the sawyer. I found the piece shown in Plate 25 lying by the roadside. It looks like the feet of an elephant and needs no carving.

In the interests of finding out what would happen in a transition from bronze to wood, I carved a version of 'The Back' by Matisse, the Impressionist painter, who created a total of seventy bronzes between 1905–11 and 1925–30. As will be seen in the plates on pages 67–70 the artist progressively reduced the muscular features by his own system of analysis. In the carved version I did exactly the same, but to a lesser degree, basing the carving on Matisse's first version but adding a broken wall in preference to his solid

24 'Jousting Horse' by the author.
Pine. 11 in. × 4 in. *Stained and waxed.*
Photograph by Derek Gabriel.

25 *Nature herself created this suggestion of the feet of an animal Holly wood. Photograph by Derek Gabriel.*

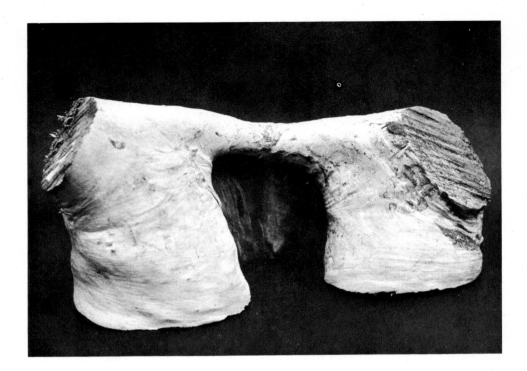

background. While experimenting with finishes, I used a small but powerful blowtorch to char the wall. During the finishing process, the nude was left unstained but polished. In time I shall do other carvings in the series to make up a quartet of panels.

Although the abstract has its own importance and is invigorating, traditional design should not be missed by the beginner. It is good practice to carve the folds of drapery, create period figures and explore the work of centuries. I am attempting to do this in a large relief panel, 'London – Middle Ages', using an old and somewhat temperamental drawing board, discovered amongst some rubbish. The figures themselves were not drawn as a group, but came from books on costume. Each figure is being given a different personality, and the skyline will be taken from an old print which shows Tudor architecture. I am adding some background grooving because I want to accentuate the flowing garments of the figures. As with all carvings there are various imperfections, but these are due mainly to the nature of the wood, which has a very uneven grain. (See p. 72).

Anthropology has already been mentioned as a prime source for ideas, but I would like to add archaeology, particularly Egyptian. Many of the murals and relief carvings in the tombs of the Pharaohs lend themselves to adaptation, especially for figure carving, because the perspective seems to benefit from a treatment in wood as regards grain and figuring.

One of the richer sources for the carver is the strong primitive sculpture of Mexico from 1800 B.C. to A.D. 2000, when the period produced grotesque figures and shapes which are not found elsewhere in 'primitive' art. The carving of the faces in particular is a good exercise, especially in the hard woods such as teak, ebony and oak, which somehow seem to match the period. (See Plates 29A and B).

The ancient Maya culture, ranging from Yucatan in the north to Honduras in the south, is not very rich in figures, and the accent is mainly upon architecture, but the treatment of the heads, human and symbolic, in surviving figures suggests that something may be gained from their study for the sake of features and the treatment of the hair. (See Plate 30C.)

66

26 *'The Back' by Henri Matisse.*
These four stages of sculpture
represent one of the few examples of
progressive abstract. By courtesy of the
Tate Gallery, London.

27   'Nude and Wall of War' by the author. Pine. 10½ in. × 12½ in.

28A The riffler in use on 'London – Middle Ages' to complete the ridges which were first cut and shaped with gouge and veiner.

28B The small gouge in use on 'London – Middle Ages' to form the ridges.

A wide selection of Aztec sculpture is suitable for dimensional carving, but my own choice would be 'Coatlicue as a young woman' (see Plate 30B). The Aztec mask shown at 30A, page 73 represents the god, Xipetotec, and here again the transition to wood might be an interesting exercise.

For the treatment of the symbolic figure in wood, African art cannot be bettered. Although these accomplished artists, located in the main in West Africa and Yorubaland, have used bronze as a medium, the ready availability of wood has made them into a race of wood carvers. Over the centuries they have evolved their own powerful and often sophisticated school of carving, which is now part of their culture. The carving is of the greatest delicacy, as in the small bust, Plate 31, which originated in the Benin region. The carver's work on the towering feather head-dress is absolutely symmetrical and is all the more remarkable for the fact that it was done with improvised tools.

African influence is perceptible in European carving, strange as it may seem. The elongation of the limbs and the exaggerated postures which typify African carvings are found in some contemporary European work. You have only to examine the work of Henry Moore (see page 32) and Alberto Giacometti to see the evidence for this.

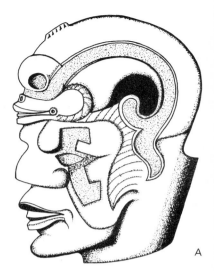

> 'One of the first principles of art so clearly seen in primitive work is truth to material; the artist shows an instinctive understanding of his material, its right use and possibilities. Wood has a stringy, fibrous consistency and can be carved into thin forms without breaking, and the Negro sculptor was able to free arms from the body, to have a space between the legs and give his figures long necks when he wished.'
> (*Henry Moore on Sculpture* edited by Philip James – quoted from the July/August 1967 Marlborough Fine Art Ltd catalogue of their Moore exhibition.)

It has often been said that a dominant characteristic of African carving is its 'childishness', a remarkable absence of self-consciousness, which is found in the drawings of very young children of any race. The African carver appreciates volume and surface, he avoids the purposeful use of space as a rule, and the face generally points forwards. These facts should be useful to teachers.

After this survey of some of the sources of design, it is as well to consider what design actually is. For a start, it should be understood that it is not ugliness, even allowing for the time-worn cliché that beauty is in the eye of the beholder. On this basis design can easily be bizarre, even startling or outrageous, but if it is good design and it has cohesion and it manages to hang together, then it should succeed in holding its own. When you are carving and the design is basically bad, or it takes a turn for the worse, you will then feel your confidence ebbing away until you finally arrive at what can only be described as a sickening moment when you know that you cannot go on with it. In other words, the design destroys itself. This is where the so-called simple' craftsman scores over the affected dilettante, who consciously uses a contrived artifice in his carving. In his book, *Traditional Country Craftsmen* (Routledge and Kegan Paul, 1965), J. Geraint Jenkins lists the three differences between the craftsman and the factory worker as follows: (1) The craftsman is able to marry beauty and utility. He is able to combine good taste and usefulness; (2) The true craftsman does not depend on complex machinery and equipment to complete his work; (3) The true craftsman is not only able to work in an ancient tradition, but he is able to build on the foundation of history. The past provides a solid basis for his work.

More than ever before in the history of mankind we need things which are good to look at, good to use and satisfying to handle. This alone makes a case for the pursuance of wood carving.

It is not enough merely to 'do a carving'. If it is to become imbued with life, then you must have a good reason for doing it in the first place. The attitude of the individual carver to this may vary. Some utilize their own symbolism, others prefer to exploit the contours of the piece, others exploit the beauty of the wood figuring. But regardless of outlook and opinion, all manage to bring new life to the wood.

29 *Two warrior heads, derived from ('A') a basalt axe of the Vera Cruz culture, ('B') An effigy vessel of the Toltec period.*

30A *Mask representing the god Xipetotec. Aztec.*

B

C

But what *is* design? This question cries out for an answer, and it can be boiled down to a series of statements. . . .

Carving design embodies curved and crooked lines. Boredom is inherent in some straight lines, especially when they form a severe frame, although this does not apply to carved friezes and borders which do run in straight lines and are a necessary part of the design.

By this time it is obvious that space, known as 'the spatial factor', does play a distinctive part in carving, and this is shown in Gothic pierced carving of screens in great cathedrals. Space has been recognized in art for thousands of years. In more practical terms, when a space is divided so that one part is more than half and less than two-thirds of the whole, the division is immediately acceptable. But a great deal must depend upon the focus of interest, and for this reason it is always a good idea to make a number of different working drawings of the same idea. They should not be line drawings. Rather, shading should be used to indicate possible undercutting, where planes will fall and curved surfaces occur, for degrees of depth are part of the carver's stock-in-trade, and they can be seen at play on the surface of a finished carving when it is placed in the right relation to a source of light. Unfortunately, though many carvings in museums and public collections are superbly placed in spacious glass cases or on highly polished plinths, the effect is destroyed by an overall distribution of daylight or insensitive shadowless fluorescent lighting. These carvings are seldom seen to full advantage. It is impossible to particularize on this point of correct display, because each carving is different. When you are designing a carving, it is a good idea to remember that deep cutting gives a high relief and shallow cutting creates just the reverse. This is the main reason why I advocate the use at close quarters of a small, medium-power desk-lamp during the carving. It can be moved round from time to time to judge the effect, and the wood carved for the best results. For much the same reason you should always stand back from a carving as you proceed with the work, looking at it from different angles to consider how one part of it influences the other.

Balance is very important, of course, and in the main it is achieved without conscious effort. It may be bisymmetric or occult. Bisymmetric, which is opposed by symmetric, comprises an arrangement on either side of a vertical axis, and it is the basis of much classical design. Symmetrical design, on the other hand, is arranged on each side of two or more axes. Occult balance means the balance on each side of a fulcrum of two unequal factions in relation to the centre.

It may appear difficult to relate rhythm and movement to carving, which is ostensibly static, but this is not the case, for a good carving has lines which guide the eye, and this is the meaning of movement.

Rhythm, on the other hand, is represented by the repetitious carving seen in a border relief, but it is also seen in the apparently clumsy and awkward African primitives. You have only to look at the huge Easter Island monoliths to see it, too. A visual exploration of rhythm, movement and form appears on pages 76–103, but this is only the beginning. The rest is personal to the carver.

Every carver should attempt to carve different designs drawn from a wide variety of sources in order to understand that style and design can be synonymous. The hallmark of a nation, a culture, is its art, not its politics. Here are some notes to assist identification, but the serious student is referred to specialist books on each of the periods.

The prehistoric Greeks utilized the laurel and the olive. The olive was for peace, and the vine, with grape and ivy, was carved into drinking vessels as a homage to Bacchus.

B   *Coatlicue, goddess of the earth, who summarizes the cosmology of Aztec beliefs. She is here represented as a young woman.*
C   *Stucco head. Maya, classical period.*

Festoons of fruit, the skulls of animals, candelabra and the mystical tripod were carved by the Romans, often with rosettes and figures.

The Egyptians carved in ebony, cinnamon and redwood, and have the distinction of having created the forerunner of the chair, which was a stool with arms and a back. Their carving was delicate, with elements of fantasy and homage to their gods. In the Louvre in Paris is a perfume spoon, formed by a young girl swimming, her body being the container for fragrant oils.

In the civilization of Crete from 3000 B.C. the carver worked chevrons, spirals of some intricacy and rosettes into his designs.

Greek art brought to carving flowers like the woodbine and acanthus leaves, human beings, feathers, fish and pure geometrical designs. It is interesting to note that the earliest Greek carving was done in wood and this, in turn, led to carving in stone in the round as distinct from relief.

In 300 B.C. the art of China and India included a great deal of wood carving, and the motifs embraced both animal and human figures, flowers and leaves, much of it in the form of story-telling panels. The art of India has a considerable history of influence, dominated by the New Brahmin period (A.D. 647–1250), but with the Mohammedan conquest came the fantastic figures, horsemen, griffins, multi-limbed deities and sub-deities, and a multitude of dream-like monsters. The ornament is both disciplined and undisciplined, and a great deal of it defies description in mere words.

The Celtic art forms a distinctive period, and it is in the main composed of birds and animals in a fine tracery. There is, too, a richness of foliage with a suggestion of post-ninth-century Roman influence. Although very few examples of wood carving have survived, there is little doubt that the Celts were carvers for decorative and utilitarian purposes.

Mayan, Aztec and Inca art represents something quite apart from the recognized schools. Mayan was at its height during the sixth century A.D. Cortez, who forced Christianity on the Mexican civilization, also destroyed an entire art tradition. Another conqueror, Pizarro, looted Peru for gold, and in so doing he destroyed many examples of Inca art. At best our records are fragmentary.

The movement of styles across wide areas of the world constitutes a study on its own. The Romanesque, which started in Italy, England, France and Germany, sprang from religious roots after the collapse of the Roman Empire. From the monasteries of the Benedictines came carvings which bore a strong suggestion of the Orient, and at the same time Western Europe was invaded by Persian art. The so-called Norman Style of 1066 exemplified the Romanesque influence, and out of it grew Gothic, which is a mixture of Oriental and Roman, as seen in the carving of flora and cusped forms. Although Gothic architecture was in transition, the use of carving in furniture came forth. An added richness came with the Renaissance of the fourteenth century, creating Italian-inspired forms of furnishing. In France it was married to the Gothic, and it reached England in 1519. By the time James I was on the throne there were the beginnings of the Later Renaissance. Furniture was heavily decorated, sometimes very crudely but with originality, though there had been a decline aided by Queen Elizabeth's refusal to use Flemish furniture. The Jacobean, rich and wholly original, was supplanted by the plainer designs forced by Cromwell's rule. Inevitably, the tone of the Queen Anne period had to grow worse before it improved with the advent of the Georgian, which lasted from 1714 to 1830, representing one of the golden ages of carving in the embellishment of domestic furniture. By 1738 Thomas Chippendale was offering finely made furniture, and he, together with the Adam Brothers, Sheraton and Hepplewhite laid the foundations of the English Style.

31 *An ebony bust from Benin, West Africa. 9½ in. high. Author's collection. Photograph by Derek Gabriel.*

In America carving has always been strongly decorative as a result of the waves of immigrants, and there are parallels with English and Continental styles, although the recognized time scale runs from Gothic, Queen Anne, Italian Renaissance, Spanish Mission and neo-Classic – a mixture of many tastes. The great American craftsmen who utilized carving in the embellishment of their designs included John Elliott, James Gillingham, John Goddard, Jonathan Gostelowe, Samuel McIntire, Benjamin Randolf, Thomas Tufft and Duncan Phyfe – individualists to a man.

*   *   *

The illustrations that follow this section have been drawn from a wide variety of styles and periods. It will be seen at once that the majority of them are not wood-carvings, but they are offered as inspirational starting-points.

A

32 This series of motifs, drawn from Oriental sources, can be adapted for relief or pierced carvings, and they are particularly useful for the young carver who is still feeling his way. It is a good idea to start with the straight-edged designs, and later attempt the curved ones.

B

C

77

D

E

33 (next page) *Motif for a decorative panel or general ornamentation, incorporating the beauty of the curve.*

34 *Stylized birds taken from African pottery decoration.*

35 *Chinese version of a bird suitable for relief carving.*

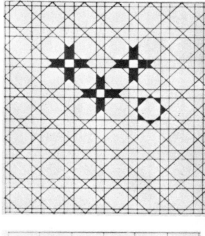

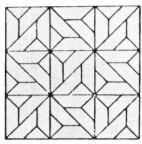

36 *How to evolve formal design on a grid, using straight lines and curves to build patterns for carving. The curved shapes are taken from Nature.*

37 *The Babylonian style of relief, full
of detail, provides instruction in relief
carving. In particular, the curved lines
lead to a rhythm of the whole. From
the Palace of Nimrud.*

38 'The Kiss' by Constantin Brancusi
(1876–1957) *was carved in limestone
in* 1908. *It is a delightfully warm
composition, dimensional and full of
expression. Philadelphia Museum
of Art.*

39   *Pennsylvania German wood*
carving design, 1745.

40   *Santo Domingo, Nicaragua, folk*
designs which lend themselves to
adaptation for carving.

84

41 *An ancient Christian symbol, the fish and the Cross.*

42 *A native wood carving from New Guinea. It is particularly ingenious from a design point of view with the two emaciated birds supporting the central figure.*

43   *Two examples of early Mexican
art. The contrast is provided by the
impression of death in basalt (left) and
grief (right). Note the simplicity of line
and the play of light on the features.*

44 *The plumed serpent which decorates the Pyramid of Quetzalcoatl, Mexico, demonstrates how an almost geometrical development can create emotion, in this case savage aggression.*

45 *A fifteenth-century plumed coyote of the Aztec culture in the Valley of Mexico. A typical geometrical arrangement of grooves and furrows.*

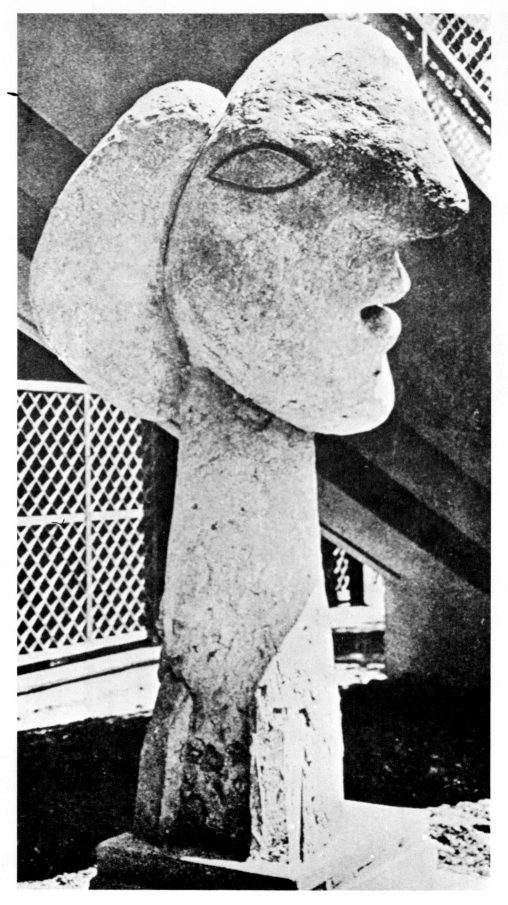

46 *'Head of Woman' by Picasso.*
1932. Cement. 57½ in. *Musée*
Grimaldi, Antibes.

90

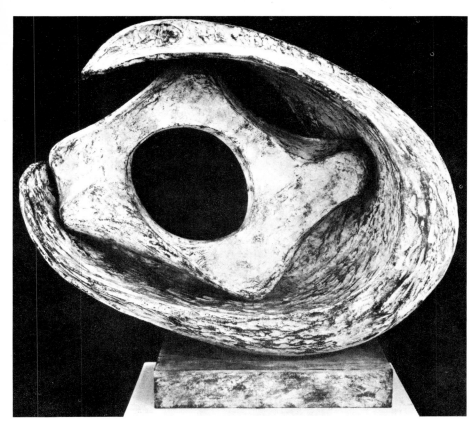

47 'Carved Form with Inner Form-
Anima' by Barbara Hepworth. Bronze.
Glynn Vivian Art Gallery, Swansea,
Glamorgan.

48 'Two Figures (Menhirs)'. Teak.
1954–5. By Barbara Hepworth.
S. B. Smith Collection, Chicago.

49 *A marble lion on Delos in the Cyclades. The line is perfect, the posture arresting. This type of ancient sculpture adapts well for wood carving.*

50 *A fifth-century Greek bronze finial form from a chariot. British Museum, London.*

51 *Demosthenes (384–322 B.C.), the Athenian orator. The line of the head and execution of hair and beard are superb.*

93

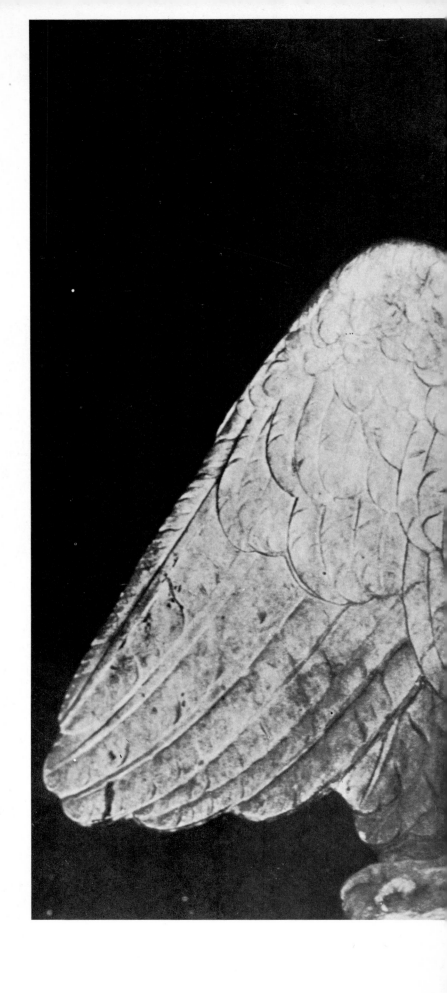

52 *Composition for a carved eagle,
based on the Roman emblem.*

95

53 *Mars, god of war (fourth century B.C.) A jubilant composition with firm lines imparting grace.*

54 *The goddess Roma, her helmet decorated with Romulus and Remus, founders of the Eternal City.*

55   *A circular motif from an Etruscan terracotta vase.*

56   *Aristion – a marble funerary stele. An interesting observation of the human form.*

57A   *'Fish' by Brancusi is another example of the curve, done in grey marble. The keynote is simplicity. 1930. Museum of Modern Art, New York.*

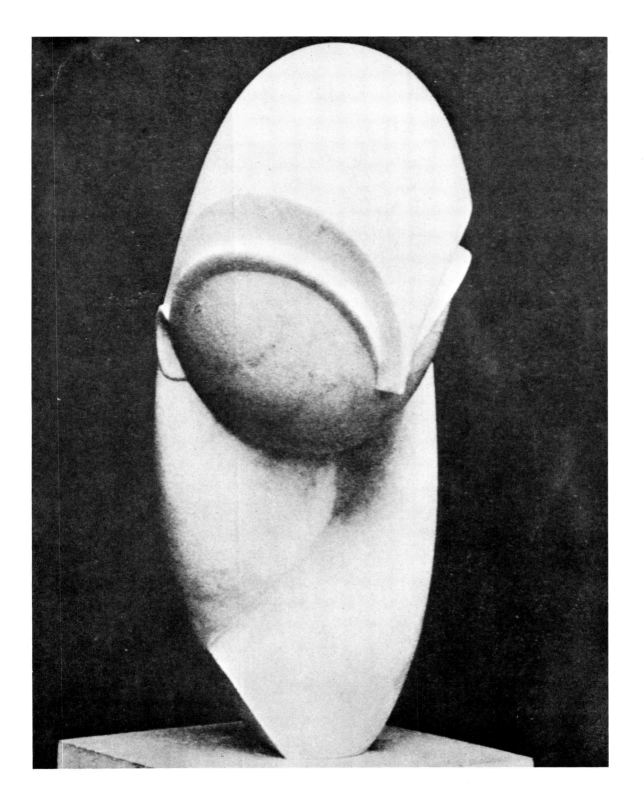

57B Brancusi's 'Mlle Pogany', done
in marble, is a first class example of the
use of the curve — eloquent,
compressed into sly characterization
and in itself an inspiration.
Tate Gallery, London

58 *'Internal and External Forms' by Henry Moore, 1953–4. One of the finest of all modern pieces. Albright-Knox Art Gallery, Buffalo, U.S.A.*

59 *'Winged figures' by Lynn Chadwick, 1955. A striking example of sharp and acute angle in a dramatic composition.*

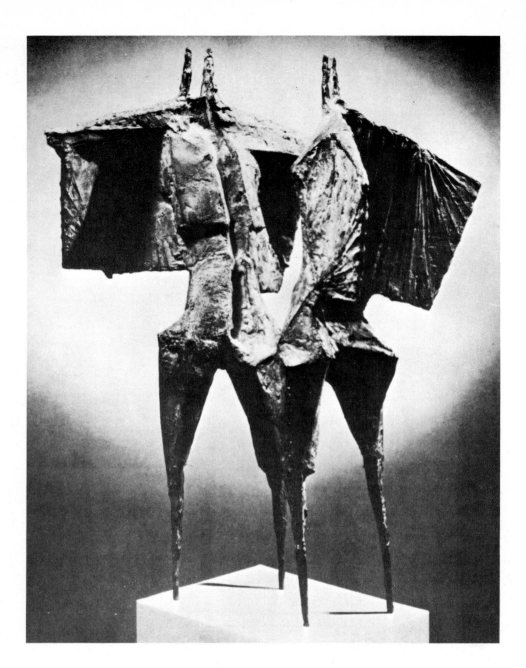

61   *A carved wood war god from New Guinea.*

60   *'One and Others' by Louise Bourgeois is a unique modern wood sculpture. The artist is greatly influenced by plant forms. 1955. Whitney Museum of American Art, New York.*

62 *'Deployed Form' by Vojin Bakic is a geometrical form in plaster.* 1958. *Drian Gallery, London.*

63 *Seated figure done in clay,* 4 in. *high. The interesting aspect of this figure is that the head has been deformed, giving a hint of the abstract and influencing the rest of the figure.*

6

Transferring the Design to Wood

Although we do not know for sure, it is likely that the earliest carvers did not play about with design as we understand it, but merely chalked a rough outline on the surface of the material and during the working with their tools allowed some inherent artistic sense to take over. It is really remarkable that many of the earliest and most primitive carvings can still say something to us across the years, yet still have a keynote of clarity, and this is particularly true of the great area of Oceania, all 463,000 square miles of it, which has produced carvings unequalled in richness, imagination and complex detail. Yet this great body of work, to be seen in museums and special collections throughout the world, was done with few tools, and the craftsmen approached the raw material without any preliminary marking or planning. Few carvers in the western hemisphere have this gift. A number of preliminary drawings must be done, failing which the work is in gestation through rough sketches. Much depends on the sort of person you happen to be, but it may be interesting to compare Henry Moore's sketches opposite with your own idea of a working drawing. In the end it does not really matter very much whether your first ideas are summed up in a few flat-looking lines or a drawing with much more substance with subtle shading and cross-hatching.

104

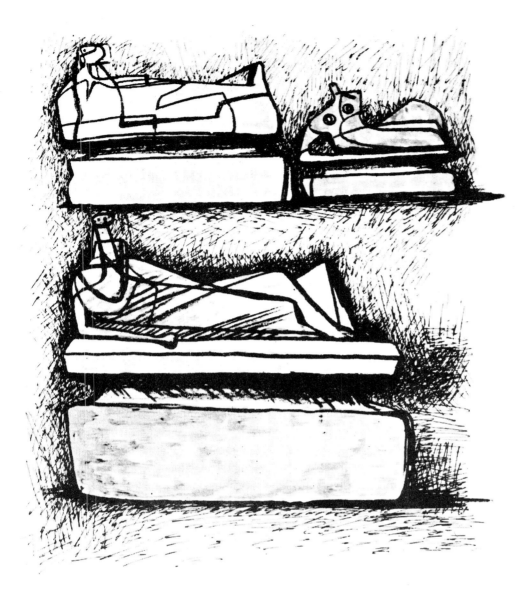

64   *Henry Moore's working sketches for 'Three Reclining Figures',* 1960; With acknowledgements to Marlborough Fine Arts Ltd., London.

What *is* important is to condition your mind to the potential *being* of the carving. For instance, if you were to consider an abstract carving, your idea might start from the premise of a certain shape, and you might not need any drawings at all, because you could 'see' the shape in the wood. In one way, this commits you to the carving and it may become too inflexible for artistic comfort. On the other hand, supposing you were to hesitate before going ahead? You could make a few exploratory drawings, the roughest sketches. The flexibility of the pencil combines with the possibility of shape variation, and before you know it, some infinitely interesting possibilities may emerge. It is worth trying. See overleaf.

What we now have to discover is how to move the guide lines of the working sketch from the paper to the wood itself. It is common enough to find that even the simplest sketch will alter ever so slightly during the transition. The actual method will be considered later on, but first of all we should consider how best to make the 'translation' of a sculpture in stone or metal into wood, as with 'The Back' by Matisse on pages 67–70. For initial working purposes you will first of all need a drawing, because a photograph will not enable you to get the 'feel' of the line. Do not confuse

105

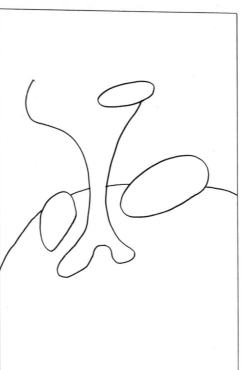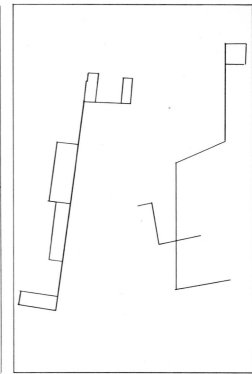

65   *Some rough exploratory sketches.*

this with skilled copying. Rather, it is a matter of interpretation. The business of exploring the line will suggest the changes and adaptations necessary to the transition.

We will assume that you are now faced with a photograph which is five inches square. The wood which you have already selected is nine inches square. Regardless of the method of reproduction, it is perfectly obvious that an overall enlargement will increase not only the length of the work but also the width.

The essentials of a photograph can be moved over to a sheet of drawing paper in one of several ways, by the use of the pantograph or by projection. The pantograph is like a section of trellis work and you can buy one from any drawing office supplier. On one end is the pointer and on the other a lead or a pencil held in a sleeve. In the middle section are screws passing through holes in the arms to adjust the scale. As pantographs are available in different sizes, this gives the carver a wide choice of scales, because the instrument not only enlarges, it also reduces.

The method of using the pantograph is simple enough, but beginners often run into difficulties for various reasons. If you are using the smaller sized pantograph, which enlarges up to about six times, the instrument will probably fit on to a dining table. Sometimes, however, the design is such that it will enlarge to such a size that the table will be too small for the operation. If you have a perfectly smooth floor – not the carpet – this is where the job can be done. For the medium sized enlargement of small working sketches a big drawing board is generally ideal. In any case, the serious carver should possess a proper board for rough sketches. It is one of the tools of the trade.

106

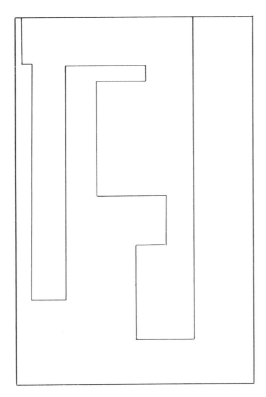 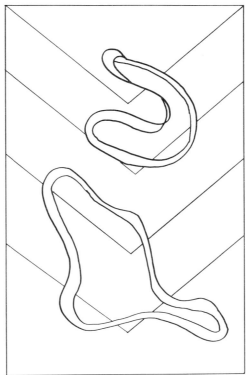

The original to be enlarged or reduced is then pinned down very firmly with mapping pins, and the pantograph is positioned in such a way that the metal pointer, or scriber, can move and swing quite freely over the entire area of the material to be enlarged or reduced. A plain sheet of cartridge paper or tracing medium is then tacked down under the drawing point of the pantograph.

The actual drawing is done by keeping your eyes fixed on the scriber and guiding it by holding the drawing point down on the plain paper with your right hand. It is a little like drawing by remote control. As the point of the scriber passes over the original, the copy will begin to appear on the blank sheet. Do not expect to attain a firm and well resolved line for a start, because an element of nervousness will enter into it. But as long as the scriber follows the original line, you cannot go wrong. If a medium to hard lead is used, the wavering line can be retouched and given boldness after all the essentials are on paper, and any shading can be inserted freehand.

Another method of enlarging an original is by squaring it, a process probably familiar to most readers of this book. You simply trace the original through a sheet of transparent graph paper, and then draw an equal number of squares each larger in the chosen proportion. Then copy the design onto the second sheet of squares, making sure that each curve crosses a line in the same place as it does on the graph paper. This is a useful method when you have a tricky outline for a dimensional carving or a piece of work containing a lot of detail.

Yet another method of starting a new carving is by creating a prototype, generally in miniature and more or less to serve as a guide for scale when you carve the final one. This is done by making a model in plaster or even soap. Almost any soap will do, but the common kitchen brand is more malleable. When working in plaster the best medium is dental plaster, which is pure white and comes in 7 lb bags as a rule. It has to be used quickly when it is mixed with water, otherwise it will set into an obstinate lump. It is a good idea to do the mixing in a rubber bowl, which can be quickly cleaned by squeezing when the plaster has set. All you have to do is crumble the plaster into enough water to make a thick creamy mix, stirring all the time with a spoon. Salt can be added if you want to accelerate setting, but do not overdo it.

You should make a box shape out of wood to correspond to the dimensions you require, but no lid or base should be added, of course. Four pieces of wood tied round with a length of string do as well as anything, and this form is set down on a sheet of glass with an oiled surface to prevent the plaster sticking as it sets. The plaster is poured into the mould very quickly and the sides of the 'box' tapped to get rid of air bubbles. If salt has been added to the mix the plaster will warm up and may even steam a little. Make sure that it is quite set before removing the wooden sides, then knock them away.

You should now have a more or less perfect cube, and this can be carved not with your regular wood carving tools but with knives and improvised tools. Old files are very useful if applied with care. In this way you create your prototype carving.

Plasticine is another useful medium for creating prototypes, also ordinary modelling clay, but care should be taken that you do not elaborate in these plastic media beyond the capacity of wood.

A personal note: although I have mentioned several methods of preparing a design for wood, the beginner cannot do better than stick to the sketchbook and pencil. For larger carvings plaster prototypes are invaluable, of course, because proportions can be judged better by this means than by sketching and working out detailed drawings. In the main, however, my personal preference is to sketch lightly on the wood itself, then get on with the carving.

7

$$\boxed{\text{Starting}}$$

'Found in a Desert' is the title of a 'mental-springboard' carving, and some
notes on the practical side of its creation may be of interest not only to other
wood carvers but also to teachers and pupils who wish to study the
evolution of an abstract.

More than twenty years ago I spent three or four years moving about in the
desert areas of the Middle East. Deserts are among the most tranquil areas
in which you could wish to dwell. They are both complicated and
uncomplicated at the same time, because they contain seas of sand, a
certain amount of thin vegetation, enormous skies, the wind and the sun.
Man is the least of it in the midst of a rich and busy insect population. I
know little about geology and geography, but in comparison with the great
age of the earth these deserts are almost new. Other things, like forests and
rivers, are of much greater age. But even if deserts are new, they have
generated a life and a personality which is peculiarly their own.

I remember moving slowly through the dunes and noticing an empty soup
tin with the red and white paper label fluttering and rattling in the breeze.
It was like a pennant or a surrealist monument to some wanderer, resting
as it did at an angle on the summit of a tall camel-back dune. As I paused to

look at it more closely, I marvelled at the appearance of what was left of the tin, peppered and pitted by millions of sand grains impinging on its surface. The tin and its condition symbolized a desert which always made its mark on anything left behind by man. Yet the most remarkable thing about sand is that regardless of how much there is of it, no two grains ever touch, because a vast air cushion is spread through it. That, at least, is the scientific view.

Moving on through a number of days and nights, I became more and more attracted to the things I found. On a beach you expect your feet to stub against objects. In a desert you expect only sand, but it is full of treasure trove and the smallest trivia contain excitement. I discovered a number of bones, none of them complete, and, later, a few artefacts, all scattered across several hundred square miles and generally visible from some distance away, because they were pure white or slightly cinnamon coloured, made so by exposure.

Crouching over them, I often found it hard to decide whether they were animal or human bones or just shards of pottery thrown up by the churning of the sand. And because I could not make up my mind, this period lodged in my mind for more than twenty years. You will now see that the subconscious of the person who is aware of line and dimension and shape and form can be a rich repository on the river bed which is constantly dredged by the conscious.

Yet the objects found in the desert were not in my conscious mind when I stood at my bench in Wales, regarding a small block of lime. The drawing was made very quickly, and this was my starting point. Although the drawing was based very approximately on a human footprint showing faintly in sand, my original intention was to carve the footprint and to bring to it certain spatial values – that is, by cutting right through the wood and making irregularly-shaped holes which would probably enhance the composition. And that was how the work was actually proceeding up to a certain point, when something caused me to stop and wait. I did not quite know which way the carving wanted to go, whether it would halt itself on the threshold of realism or march straight into the abstract.

'Abstract' is a word which frightens off many adults who suffer from withered minds, but children with imagination – and the majority possess this quality until it is knocked out of them by belligerent systems of formal education and the conditioning for a place within the economic system – take readily to it, because it is a part of their fantasy world. If you ask a child to draw, say, a 'queer animal', you generally get more than you bargained for, visually speaking, whereas an adult who has to draw a 'queer animal' might just about manage to probe only the top layer of fantasy, and this will cost him a tremendous mental effort. To explore the abstract, you need a mixture of one part intelligence to one part perceptive eye to one part the mind of a child. People who expect to comprehend what the abstract is without first knowing what actuates and energizes it often feel angry, disappointed and frustrated. Yet the child does not need to know, he is instinctively at one with it. He requires no academic explanation and no rationalization, because he dwells simultaneously in two mental countries, the country of his own imaginings which is rich and largely abstract and full of freedom, and the country of the adult, which is 'outside' territory, and noted for its controls and discipline.

As Picasso says: 'Everybody wants to understand art, why not try to understand the song of a bird?'

There is a vast difference between knowing what the abstract is and actually creating the abstract for yourself in any medium from painting to

110

carving. Putting it basically, abstract art is really a simplification, a taking-away of inessentials, a studied deduction of the superfluous. Much of the later art of Picasso is an example of this. As he said: 'We hang on to out-of-date ideas and obsolete definitions as if the role of the artist were not to supply new ones.' Whether he is modelling, sculpting, painting or making pottery and decorating it, Picasso may begin with a complexity of formal, serious or humorous lines which are then progressively reduced until only a few of the salient ones remain to capture and state the essence of the original. The child does this, too, by drawing in outline. And you also find it in some primitive carving. In all great work simplification is very noticeable and it applies strongly in wood carving.

If the teacher is endeavouring to bridge wood carving and abstract art, he will do well to ask his pupils to think first about the most important thing in a carving – the focal point. You have to educate the child to this extent, and it is a good idea to create a schema embracing a very wide field of visual studies, encouraging the child to do plenty of 'applied looking' at everything from architecture to a jam jar. Everything visual contains an essential point. At a later stage the young carver should be able to simplify his most muddled working sketches and get rid of all that fussy detail, then to 'see' the thing in the wood even before he picks up his tools and starts work.

All this may help to explain why I gravitated towards an abstract to act as a centrepiece for this book. I could quite easily have featured a number of winsome little donkeys, dogs and dolls, plaques or relief carvings of one sort or another, but the pitfall in following this course would be that someone somewhere would like them so much that they would copy them, cut for cut, and we would be back to the old-fashioned carving class in which a particular set piece was copied and re-copied until finally it had no guts left and was totally devoid of all spirit. So instead of providing the reader with simple copying pieces, I chose to evolve the abstract, 'Found in a Desert', which is illustrated in three different stages in these pages. Although I decided to do this, it does not mean that I spurn the purely figurative or representational. But in my own estimation an abstract carving can provide far greater interest and intellectual stimulation than the examination of a 'storybook' carving. Where the human mind automatically registers the proportions of a common and familiar shape, such as an animal, when it comes to the abstract, the mind must do some work for itself. If man is unable to explore, both mentally and physically, then he remains a creature in a treadmill.

Visual education has improved to such an extent since the birth of Impressionism in the mid-nineteenth century that nowadays even people who confess to no comprehension of 'modern art' will cheerfully accept the abstract on curtains, crockery and packaging, because they say that the colour and line appeal to them. A great deal of this almost automatic acceptance and appeal is connected with abstract wood carving, for in looking at it and touching it even the most non-art person will compensate for a lack of immediate understanding by an interest in the shape of the wood, its surface and proportions. And the fact that it is made from wood seems to mean something in a plastic world.

But it must be emphasized that to carve wood for the pleasure of others can be foolish and a complete waste of time. It is too much like painting for an audience. You paint or carve purely for your own pleasure and development. Commercial carvers are caught up in the thrall of trying to please everybody at the same time – the gifte shoppe touch – and it simply does not work. If a carving has any artistic value, then it will eventually attract its own audience, and even if that audience comprises a minority, then it has done its job. This fact should be brought home to any carver who wishes to explore the abstract. The work is done and the creation is created purely for its own sake. One commentator, Alfred Buhler, has said: 'Wherever carvings and paintings are produced nowadays for the commercial market, detached from their traditional function, we find that the ancient motifs and styles are almost invariably presented in a degenerate form; we have only empty shells devoid of content.'*

A word here about the carver's personal attitude to the abstract during the carving process. Working on an abstract must perforce be evolutionary. When you work representationally, on the other hand, you are virtually copying. In other words, a-dog-is-a-dog-is-a-dog-is-a-dog-is-a-dog, and nothing is going to alter that basic fact. When the dog is carved, it will look like a dog and nothing else. Conversely, abstract art does not set out with any preconceived notions, although it does have a very firm discipline. In many cases it will have a starting point, and in the case of 'Found in a Desert' it was the often amorphous white or near-white objects embedded in the sand. But there was no preconceived notion of the final shape beyond this haunting idea of animal bone or perhaps the artefact of an earlier and forgotten civilization. It was a starting point.

Despite the mention of discipline, the abstract provides the carver with a maximum mental freedom during the initial stages, although concentration is intense. Later comes the point at which the wood itself seems to take over. In the case of the present carving it happened shortly after the initial guide lines were cut away at the commencement of the midway stage. Up to that point the vague footprint idea had been the dominant theme, but now the desert took over and altered the entire course of it.

Teachers will find it useful to let young carvers have their heads in exploring ideas. It is a sorry mistake to try and persuade the child to say what he intends carving before the job is even started. Rather, ease into it gently, giving a series of informal introductory talks about the idea of the abstract, and these can easily be linked to visual instruction and full discussion.

'All our knowledge has its origins in our perceptions,' said Leonardo da Vinci, and this is the perceptual conditioning which can be given to young people.

The child should be encouraged to search the wood pile for suitable materials. Every school should have a wide choice of wood, not merely neat lumps, odd chunks and machined planks. Irregularly shaped pieces and old furniture are invaluable when it comes to working in the abstract.

Teachers will quickly discover that some young people find it difficult to 'get started' when it comes to abstract carving. This is not unusual. In the typical classroom atmosphere and environment certain children will feel self-conscious and they will fall into a group in need of firmer guidance. It may even be a good idea to allocate definite projects to these non-abstractionists, because they will probably be much happier carving animals and readily identifiable shapes. Meanwhile, those who want to carve in the abstract can carry on unaided. Speed has nothing to do with it. The slower the abstract is in evolution, the better it may turn out to be.

These ideas apply also to the adult carver, though with certain qualifications, for he is likely to be working on his own and without the benefit of explanatory talks and discussion. Consequently, adult progress may be slower, but with the influence of maturity the breakthrough to understanding will come sooner.

* Buhler: Barrow and Mountford: *Oceania and Australia*. Methuen, 1962.

The wood used for 'Found in a Desert' was lime, measuring $3\frac{1}{2}$ in. × $9\frac{1}{2}$ in. × 1 in. thick, which is a convenient size for handling and general manipulation.

Lime is a wonderful wood, as a rule devoid of knots and burls, and with a distinctively even figuring. I buy several pieces of it at once from a dealer who specializes in carving wood, and it is supplied planed and finished on all sides. As carving wood goes, lime is fairly reasonable in price, and the principal application is ecclesiastical figure carving. A certain amount of large wood sculpture in lime has been done, but seldom on a very big scale, because it is difficult to find pieces of sufficient size.

The drawing was first made on tracing cloth and then transferred to the wood, using carbon paper. I went over the outline with a felt-tipped pen to retain the boldness, whereas a fainter carbon outline would be quickly erased by handling during the preliminary carving.

At this early stage it is not unusual for a new carver to feel faint-hearted, because the lines on the wood look so bare and barren, apparently having no relationship to the carving – or any carving. The only antidote to this early negation is to press on as soon as the drawn line seems to be in the correct proportions to the dimensions of the wood. In other words, if it fits, start carving.

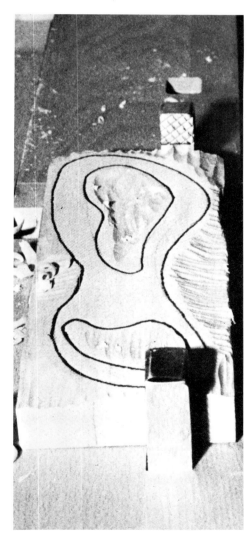

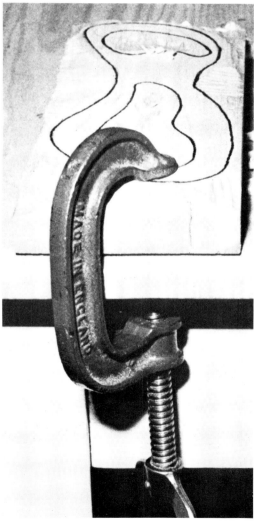

66 *Before bosting-in commences, ensure that the workpiece is held very firmly in position on the bench. There are two main methods: the pair of bench dogs in 'A' are adjusted by means of an end-vice, forming an integral part of the bench structure; or the G-cramp, as shown in 'B'.*

A

B

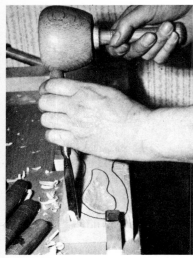

C

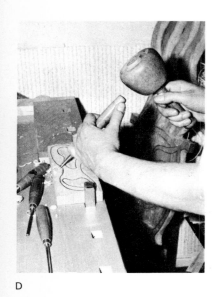

D

You can now begin the 'bosting in'. This is easy enough, because it consists of removing superfluous wood. One word of warning. In the case of an abstract, it will pay you not to remove too much wood from around the drawn outline, and the bosting in should be done only to a depth of about $\frac{1}{4}$ in. or less. Where the object to be carved is representational and more definite, and is to be shown in relief, you can go down more deeply to $\frac{1}{2}$ in. or $\frac{3}{4}$ in. If the carving is in the round, or dimensional, then the idea is to remove all 'outside' wood.

Bosting in is done with a gouge. Depending upon the size of the wood and the margins, one of the wider gouges should be used for the sake of speed and efficiency. If you use a small gouge this part of the carving will take too much time. In such a case the young carver will be bored, because it can be very tedious.

The gouge should not be driven too deeply into the wood, Try using it in different ways, by pushing, by striking the handle with the palm of the right hand (except in the case of the left-handed carver) and with the mallet. If you have more than one mallet, test them all for force of stroke. Previous experiments on waste wood will demonstrate the capabilities of the tools and the depth at which you can work.

For the first phase of bosting in, work with, or along, the grain to get the feel of the wood. In the case of lime, only an even pressure is needed to start the cutting action of the gouge. All cuts should be as even as you can make them. Unless the gouge is driven in at a near-vertical angle, there is practically no danger of its getting jammed in the wood, because it should cut cleanly and upwards due to its sharpened angle. But if it does embed itself in the wood it is wrong to try and force it through with a mallet, hoping that it will free itself. It will not do anything of the sort, it may damage the wood, and it will probably go deeper. In your efforts to free it with a bull-in-a-china-shop technique you may snap the steel. The correct way to free an embedded tool is to cut down towards the point with a chisel, carefully removing the wood as you go. An accomplished carver never finds himself in this irritating predicament.

Bosting in should be done all the way round the drawn outline at a distance of about $\frac{1}{4}$ in. Unless the work is being done in hard wood there is no need to use the mallet, although this is a good chance to get in some practice with it.

Always work outwards and away from the drawn outline, never towards it. A sharp gouge can slip and run straight across the drawn section, neatly bisecting it.

Bosting in should be done with clean even strokes, making a series of adjacent troughs, or grooves, in the wood. If you used your broadest gouge for the first removal of the top surface, go round it again, this time using the medium sized gouge to narrow down the troughs. After this has been done, do yet another round with the smallest gouge. You should try and space the troughs as evenly as possible, because this is good practice with the tools, and you will quickly find out how to control the action with the wrist muscles. Small faults like cuts going awry can easily be corrected by recutting the area at this stage, so you are comparatively safe.

Another thing to bear in mind is the position of your body in relation to the workpiece. Do not hunch or crouch over it, but keep the body almost upright with plenty of play on the arms and hands. When you use the mallet make sure that you plant your blows dead square on the handle.

Throughout this part of the carving the wood should be held firmly by means of a 'G' cramp or by using bench dogs (see page 113), and the cuts must be made away from your body. Another important reminder: your free hand should never rest anywhere in the path of the tool, especially when cutting across the grain, which calls for a firmer wrist control and greater force. It is not always possible to work with the grain, and this is a good opportunity to try out some cross-grain cutting.

Many absolute beginners are quick to discover the delights and the sensuous pleasures of the action of the tool as it cuts so smoothly through the wood, but when you work on a relief you must resist the temptation to go down too deeply. Contemporary carving in relief is generally very shallow in comparison with, say, the Grinling Gibbons school. On the other hand, a relief carving which is too shallow may look skimped and hurried. Somewhere between the two is the proverbial happy medium.

If a dimensional carving is being done, the bosting in consists of blocking out the main lines, first by the method already described, and then by cutting the rough outline out of the wood. It helps if you run the wood rasp round the outline for the sake of the contouring. When you are at this stage you should allow ample wood for the carving of detail.

Bosting in is generally a short process, and in commercial carving is done by an apprentice. All you are doing is cutting away unnecessary wood and throwing the outline of the carving into a kind of overall relief. If you can clearly 'see' what you are after, then the transition to the midway stage will be imperceptible. Later on, when you are more proficient, you will find it unnecessary to demarcate the boundaries in three distinct stages. Carving will then be like a single piece of music, the bosting in being the preliminary statement, leading smoothly to the centre of the work and ending with the final declaration, which is the sum total of the carving.

For the present, however, the beginner should pause when the bosting in is complete and take stock. Even at this early stage there will be the inevitable urge to put in some finishing touches – a little more wood to be removed here, a groove to be corrected there.

The appearance will be of a sharp pencilled outline on a slightly raised section of wood. You may feel that progress is slow, but the carving is, nevertheless, taking on a life of its own. During the midway stage the carver's intention is to add the flickering of existence – some new muscles, blood and sinews – and the carving will then begin to live.

8

'All the dimensions of vision are permissible.'

Picasso

Midway

Until you begin to feel integrated, or 'at home', with a carving, it is a good idea to allow a slight pause between stages to think about it. In the case of abstract carving, the wood itself begins to give indications of its coming form through the shapes and contours and the figuring. When carving straightforward figures and panels, you should not work willy-nilly on isolated sections or areas, but try and make the work grow from one definite nucleus, and this nucleus can be anywhere. It is wrong to dodge about, trying first one part and then another. Nor should you necessarily exploit the easiest section first of all. Very often the more difficult one will be the more fruitful in the long run. The point is that carving which is in progress will tend to develop from one particular centre – a generator, so to speak.

A great deal of the midway section of development of 'Found in a Desert' had to be exploratory, because I still felt uncertain which way the carving was going. In such a case it is always a good idea to restrict the number of tools in use, because limitation creates less distraction. In Micronesia and Melanesia the native craftsman still works with only one single implement, an adze with a blade made from a clam shell. In primitive

116

areas where modern carving tools have been introduced, this has not resulted in any innovations as far as style and execution are concerned. This phase of 'Found in a Desert' was done with two gouges, a corner chisel, three rifflers and a rasp, the latter being used to rough out the edges of the carving. But in comparison with the carvers of Micronesia and Melanesia I had a wealth of tools at my disposal. The only ancillary tool in occasional use was a knife with interchangeable blades, and this was brought into play to create a series of flat planes on the top edge of the carving.

One factor which may be studied at this point is the use of spatial values, situated at each end and on one side of the carving. Internal space can impart considerable strength to a carving. By opening up the material you can, so to speak, relate the front to the back and also suggest greater depth, quite apart from creating a certain unity in the form itself. The shape of the boundaries of the hole warrants special consideration, because it is here that spatial values also count. The best contemporary example is, of course, Henry Moore, whose development has also embraced the figure-within-the-figure. Apart from Moore, the sculpture of Alexandre Noll with traces of Chinese and Negro influences is an example of the spatial. Some of Nuñez del Prado's non-figurative carvings, on the other hand, utilize a spatial value without outside boundaries – large symmetrical scoops out of the wood, as in 'The Virgin'.

A

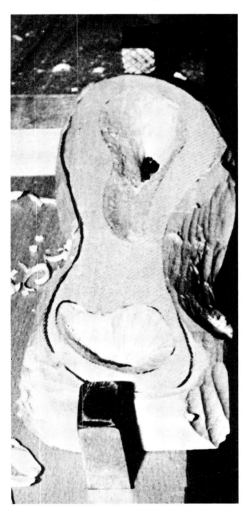

B

67 *The narrow gouge was used for working the internal hollows (as in 'A'), until the depth was satisfactory (as in 'B'), by which time most of the outside dimensions had been roughed out. Various rifflers ('C', 'D', 'E') were then used to decide the final planes which would be enhanced by light. A large riffler was also used to form the edges 'F'. Photographer: Derek Gabriel.*

The outside, or peripheral, shape of 'Found in a Desert' did not materially alter much at this stage, because I still felt the footprint idea to be apposite in view of the title. What did materialize was a series of planes at the top of the carving, done with a surgically-sharp knife which removed the wood in wafer-thin layers. At the beginning of this stage there was a thickish ridge and into this I incised gulleys and eroded deepenings which symbolized dune indentations caused by the wind working against impacted sand.

The narrow gouge was then used to shape some sharp ridges down the sides of the lower hole, and these, too, were indications of the sand ripples created by alternating winds.

The extended hole at the side of the carving was originally a plain curve, symbolizing the escarpments of the desert, but the idea then changed direction and became a wafer-thin representation of an animal bone picked clean by the dung beetles and scoured for months by the wind and sand. It was done very gradually, first using the gouge and then the knife until an ultimate thinness was reached. Then it was pierced and shaped.

In the centre of the main body is the half-concealed suggestion of a shield, obscured by a rise in the wood. What I had in mind here were the many armed campaigns of man which have come and gone, leaving the drifting sands to cover the traces of human idiocy.

After all the main cutting and shaping was done, I used both large and small, flat and curved rifflers to get rid of the upstanding wood fibres. The small curved riffler was used on the shoulders of the deep hole to improve the contours and make them more distinctive.

What happens during the midway stage of a carving is that you find a need for a certain freedom to let the wood find its own shape, and once this is sensed, progress is rapid. I think the important thing in abstract carving is not to be too retrospective or held back by your own initial conception. At best, it is only a starting point, nothing more. At the end of the middle stage all we should care about is the final evolution.

c

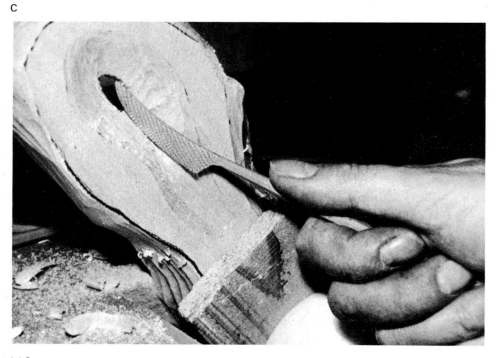

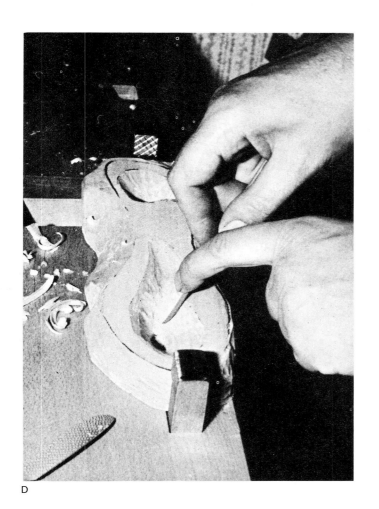

D

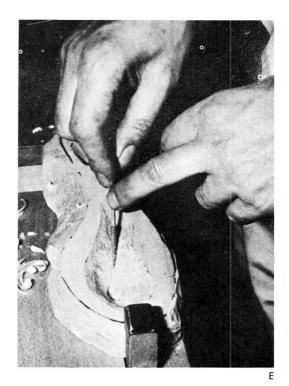

E

F

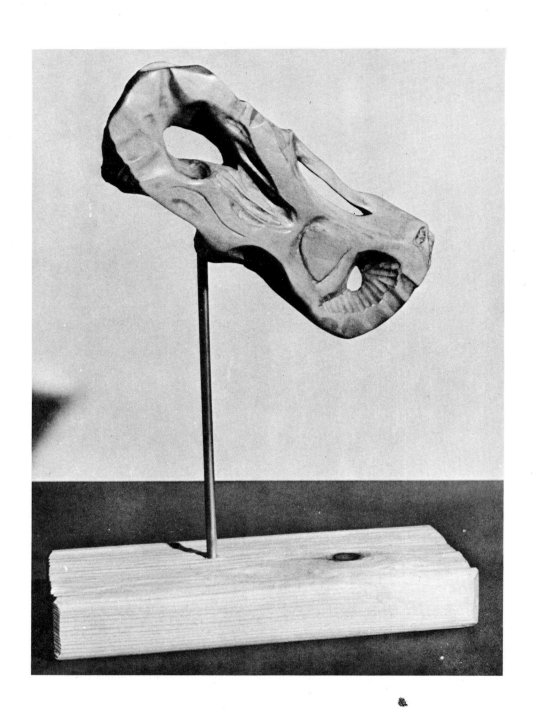

68 *'Found in a Desert' completed.*
Photograph by Derek Gabriel.

9

Completing

'An art style is not a static but a dynamic phenomenon, bound up and changing with a specific period of cultural development.'

Leonhard Adam

As the reader will know after studying Section Ten: *Finishing*, the choice of finishes is extremely wide, ranging from fuming certain kinds of wood to laying on a white, or transparent, polish: Or, of course, you can gild or polychrome your work. The final finish is extremely important when considered in relation to the actual spirit and the intention of the carving.

Many modern carvers merely rub their work over with wax and leave it at that, but I have always preferred the mellowed appearance created by a polish made from flaked orange shellac and alcohol. On a first application the orange hue may seem to be over pronounced, making the work look cheap and nasty, but later applications of the stuff plus a considerable amount of elbow grease will give the wood a burnished look.

In the case of 'Found in a Desert', the entire area was first of all wiped over quickly with a cloth soaked in a spirit-based walnut stain. This resulted in an uneven and disappointing blotchiness, so I then wiped it over with methylated spirit and treated it to a very quick bleaching, using the method described in Section Ten. It had the effect of dispersing the denser areas of the stain so that the colour now spread more or less evenly but thinly over the entire surface.

121

The carving was then allowed to dry for two days at normal room temperature, and the orange polish was applied in four thin films. The interesting thing was that the colour of the walnut stain, which is best described as rich russet, reacted, and the final effect was the mellow brown which I wanted to achieve. The stain showed through the polish. Not that it always happens this way. You just have to experiment. There are no short cuts, no set standards.

One thing did happen during the bleaching which is on my agenda for future investigation. I happened to drop some neat concentrated solution of acetic acid fifty per cent on the wood, and it created a near ashen effect on the lime, which I dispersed with water.

Preparation of the piece for finishing amounted only to the removal of loose wood fibres and the smoothing of areas which would eventually reflect the highlights after the piece was polished.

It is debatable whether any wood carver is ever truly satisfied with a finished carving, but in this case I think that I achieved almost everything I envisaged when I first examined the wood and made the drawing. But, as with many abstracts, I think that it is but one in a chain of many developments, like the Eskimo mask discussed earlier. 'Found in a Desert' could grow into a series, each one quite different but all linked together by a single thought. This is the real reason for working in the abstract. It is the personification of thought and ideas, a groping through mist to sunlight in an uninhabited country. While all who work in the abstract know this, few are able to explain it very adequately, but what I have tried to do is make my own statement about the process. Again, we can profit from studying Henry Moore's work, for he has now done more than eighty versions of the 'Reclining Nude' (see Plate 7). As his biographer, Donald Hall,* tells us, Moore would need five lifetimes to exhaust the possibilities of the figure which has already gone through the neo-Mayan, surrealist, constructivist and neo-classical. Yet this vast symphony of shapes represents variations on a single shape.

> In the beginning was the thought.

* Donald Hall: *Henry Moore*. Gollancz, 1966.

122

10

Finishing

When a carving is completed you are faced with several choices. It can, of course, be left exactly as it is, or it can be treated in a variety of ways. Some professional carvers are fierce in their denunciation of any finishing at all, but the fact remains that it enhances and beautifies the wood.

A preliminary warning: never varnish a carving. All this does is put a high gloss indiscriminately all over the surface. It is a maltreatment of the wood, sealing it off from the world. The near plastic, synthetic appearance will detract from the lines of the carving and kill the beauty of the wood. It does not necessarily apply to carvings which will be exposed to wind and weather, of course, because maximum protection should be given to prevent dampness from making the wood soggy and rot from setting in. Even so, varnishing is not strictly necessary, because a special grade of polyurethane is now obtainable, and it is vastly superior to varnish, because it gives a more striking and often a much softer look to the figuring.

Very seldom is a carving left in its natural state without any treatment at all, because the figuring of the wood will not show up without attention. After line and design, figuring is the next most important factor. For instance, some woods with a striped figuring may be used for animal carvings, and if the figuring has a role to play, then it should be brought out.

Many beginners dab on a coating of polish or some oil preparation and then feel disappointed by the lack of reaction. Similarly, many beginners mistake the quick 'mellowing' of the wood as soon as it is smeared with polish or oil, but this effect occurs only because the wood fibres are moistened, Much the same thing would happen if you were to dab on some warm water.

To achieve a successful and lasting finish a carving must be thoroughly prepared, and it is a good idea to give it a quick wash in tepid water and weak bleach, then dry it quickly in a bath towel. This cleanses the surface of the wood after carving and it gets rid of sweat and grease from the hands. Another method is to wipe the carving down with a rag moistened with methylated spirit, which is a better method.

Sandpapering has caused many arguments amongst carvers, and a great deal depends on the nature of the carving. It is not a good idea to sandpaper carvings which rely for their effect on tool marks. But other carvings are enhanced by a perfectly smooth finish, and here sandpapering is desirable. As usual, everything depends on personal preference and the nature of the carving. If a carving has to be finished in such a way as to accentuate the tool marks, no preliminaries are needed and all you use is a good wax polish. But if some areas are to radiate a sheen, then some preparation is needed and you can use various grades of sandpaper, ranging from coarse to superfine.

Sandpapering and smoothing must always be done with the grain, not against or across it, for this makes uneven scratches which are difficult to remove. In some cases they can be taken out only by resurfacing the area with carving tools or rifflers – a tedious and destructive business which may alter the nature and appearance of the carving. But if you sandpaper with the grain, then no scratching should occur, especially if you maintain the right pressure. It is not advisable to use the coarse sandpaper first in every case, because some woods abrade rapidly, and these require kinder and gentler treatment. Start with a medium grade paper and finish with the finest, the so-called 'flour' sandpaper. When using the finest grades it is a good idea to stop now and then, and blow away any surplus wood dust, which clogs the abrasive action. But make sure you do blow instead of using your fingers or a rag, because this, too, can cause scratching.

Sandpapering is not as simple as it seems. Do not emulate the carpenter and wrap the paper round a wood block, because carvings are uneven and block sandpapering will miss many areas. But if you can feel the contours of the carving with your fingers through the sandpaper, then each area will be smoothed and made ready for the next phase of finishing. With use sandpaper becomes soft and flexible, and it is still possible to go on using it, because this gives a sheen to the wood. My methodical wife labelled a small box 'Bits of Sandpaper', and this has become one of my handiest accessories.

You will find on the market ready-made tungsten-carbide blocks, which are supposed to be for wood smoothing, but they are no good to the carver, because they are hard and inflexible, and will score even lignum vitae and ebony.

Garnet paper, which costs more and lasts longer, is used by many carvers, and the fine grades are distinguished by these numbers: $\frac{1}{2}$, 0, 3/0, 5/0 and 8/0. Although I have advised against the use of a wooden block, garnet paper can be wrapped round a small cork block and it will give satisfactory results, because the cork 'gives' to the surface of the carving. It is best to use a No. 0 grade, and then, when sanding is completed, use a slightly damp cloth to wipe the surface. This will bring up any loose fibres which have been lifted by the garnet paper. The next application should be with No. 5/0, and this will detach the fibres which would otherwise be a nuisance during polishing.

In another section of this book I mentioned the use of power tools. Some steel burrs can be used to smooth down areas of a carving, but there is always a danger of breaking the surface and roughing it up, even when the drill is running at its slowest speed. Some woods will take the burr in a left-to-right motion, and provided you do not use too much pressure it can give a pleasing appearance.

69 *Carvings by Guy Ngan of New Zealand. This carver studied at the Royal College of Art, London, under Professor David Pye. The work shows an unusual originality, utilizing sand blasting as a finish. The wood is Pinus radiata, and in Ngan's range it is used for decorative purposes in hotels, shops and houses. Photographs by courtesy of Guy Ngan. See also next page.*

A

B

C

D

E

F

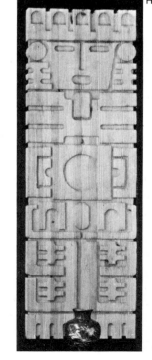

H

G

A   4 in. × 1 in. *thick.*
B   24 in. × 24 in.
C   3 in. × 1 in. *thick.*
D   4 in. × 1 in. *thick.*
E   36 in. × 2 in. *thick.*
F   6 in. × 1 in. *thick.*
G   3 in. × 1 in. *thick.*
H   72 in. × 2 in. *thick.*

126

Power tool carvers may well feel tempted to use a lambswool polisher to finish a carving, because it appears to be speedy and efficient, but unless it is kept constantly on the move, it may create frictional heat and raise blisters in shellac polishes and these, in turn, can inflict dark scars on the wood beneath.

To return to the finish itself, the beginner should start by studying the effect of boiled linseed oil on, say, a piece of carved lime. When carved the lime will look yellowish to near-white, and in time it will increase in yellowness. But if you oil polish it, this will progressively bring out the figuring, and after further applications it will grow darker.

One method of oil polishing is to brush on the boiled linseed oil for a week or two, and then use a preparation consisting of one-eighth of turpentine to boiled oil. The oil should be heated to just below boiling point, removed from the stove and the turpentine (or turpentine substitute) added. The mixture should be well stirred and allowed to cool before application.

The best way of doing it is to put it on with a stiffish brush, forcing it down into the grain. Brushing with a liberal quantity of oil-and-turpentine mixture can be done daily for six weeks. It takes only a few minutes. Do not soak the carving at every application, but see that a film is brushed into the wood until it disappears. After a time the wood will reach saturation point, and no further brushing is necessary. Lay the carving on a wad of newspapers while the internal chemistry of oil and turpentine and resin continues. Quite suddenly – and I have known this to happen overnight – you will find the appearance of the wood changing. It will begin to look older, more mature. Within a few days residual oil will dry, and you can then begin to polish it, using a piece of soft, clean, unbleached linen. Do not apply any more oil and turpentine mixture at this stage. Elbow grease and a firm pressure are needed. At first nothing much seems to happen, but after some persistent rubbing you will notice that the linen is taking up a minute amount of surplus oil, which is exuded by the wood pores. After this deposit has come away, encouraged by the friction and warmth of your hands, apply a few spots of boiled linseed oil, and this will be absorbed very quickly. The final appearance will give a warm sheen.

The only drawback to this method of oil finishing is that it shows up cutting faults in all those awkward places where the chisel or gouge just stopped short, perhaps held back by an area of cross grain. The result is generally a dirty looking mark, like a pencil scribble or an indentation. It is no good trying to remove this while the oil is still soaking into the wood, because all the fibres are soft and they will probably tear further, making the mark even more noticeable. All this potential irritation can be avoided if preparation is thorough in the first place.

In some parts of the Continent commercial carvers use a variation of the oil finish technique. The carving is prepared, then lightly brushed over with a coating of boiled linseed oil. It is floated in a container of the same oil, which is slowly brought to simmering point and then lowered. After three such 'cookings' the carving is left soaking for twenty-four hours, then removed and wiped dry. Exposure to light and air for another day or two will result in a mellowed appearance. This type of oil bath treatment can be used on both soft and hard woods.

Yet another variation, useful for small relief panels, which enables the carver to graduate the development of an oil-polish finish, is to line a baking tin of sufficient size with aluminium foil. Boiled linseed oil is poured into the tin and the carving placed face down in it. The carving should not be completely covered. You can treat small dimensional carvings by this method if the piece is turned from time to time. Various experiments with

70 *This piece was carved from lime,*
$9\frac{1}{2}$ *in.* × $3\frac{1}{4}$ *in.* × 1 *in.* *thick, merely to*
demonstrate various finishes. The
background was bleached by the
method explained on page 134.
The face was matt finished with
orange shellac and alcohol, and the
scarf was stained with light oak and
over-polished with the same polish
used for the face. Although not shown
in this illustration, the sides were black
polished. In the collection of Mrs.
A. C. Meadowcraft. Photograph by
Derek Gabriel.

different heat levels suggest that what is called a 'cool oven' (approximately 200° to 250°F.) provides the best effect. The oil should reach an equitable temperature within ten or fifteen minutes, and then begin to react on the wood. Frequent inspection will determine the degree of mellowing required and the process can be halted at any time. It is important to cover the surface of the carving with aluminium foil when it is not immersed in the oil to avoid starting flaws and cracking, and the heat should not be permitted to build to a great height. This method, used in conjunction with others to damage the surface of the carving and simulate age, is used by many of the most accomplished forgers of 'medieval' carvings in Italy. It was originated as far as we know by a man called Alceo Dossena, who specialized in the fabrication of church carvings which looked even more ancient than the originals – if originals existed.

Nowadays a great range of polishes and finishes are available in a made-up form, and most of these are admirable if you want first-class results for a negligible outlay. However, many carvers prefer to conduct their own experiments, and it is often the fluke which is the best and most satisfying. The following notes will be found useful:

French Polish

This can be bought in a made-up form, but it is cheaper to make it yourself. It is applied over a grounding of raw – not boiled – linseed oil, and no filler should be used on the grain, because the oil itself will fill the pores. It is a good idea to rub the carving over with shavings and sawdust, because this helps to fill the grain.

The polish is made very easily, and it consists of a mixture of $\frac{3}{8}$ lb of orange shellac to each pint of alcohol. It is not merely sloshed on to the wood and rubbed in. You have to make a lint-free pad, and I recommend old and well-washed sheets for this purpose. The inside of the linen rubber should be filled with scraps of the same material, and a few drops of oil should be poured over them for lubrication.

Use a smooth motion, up and down the carving, not across the grain. As soon as the rubber seems to be holding, or binding, on the surface of the wood, stop polishing and renew the polish, adding more oil to the inside of the rubber.

Do not make the mistake of trying to polish the entire surface at one attempt, but work in overlying areas. Never allow the rubber to stop or slow down on the surface, because this can cause patchiness.

After three or four applications, when the polish seems to be taking, stop and rub it down thoroughly with a very fine sandpaper. Now resume polishing. You can apply any number of coats of French polish, and each will give a higher lustre than the previous one. . . . This reminds me of a friend who became so engrossed in the process that he applied seventy-two coats before his troubled wife pleaded with him to stop. The piano stool he was polishing put the piano in the shade – and the piano itself was new.

Sheraton's Polish

This was originated by the famous English furniture maker, who lived from 1750 to 1806.

Beeswax is absorbed by turpentine to form a thick paste. Using a cork, you should work it into the surface of the wood. For the final polish very fine brick dust is sifted through a piece of silk on to the wood, then rubbed with a cloth.

Here is a modification of the process: sand the wood surface, then wipe it over with a damp cloth to raise the loose fibres. Rub it down again with fine sandpaper. Now mix boiled linseed oil with turpentine in an equal proportion. Place the carving in a warm room, and heat the mixture to simmering point, then, while it is still hot, rub it on, using a soft cloth. After eight to twelve coats and an equal number of rubbings, the result should be a lasting finish, which can be waxed.

Fuming oak or chestnut

This was done originally by suspending the finished carving in a stable to absorb ammonia fumes given off by the horse urine in the stalls below. The chemical reaction of the fumes on the wood resulted in a darkening – the typical appearance of oak or chestnut. Nowadays the carver would be hard pressed to find stables and a sufficient number of urinating horses, but he can build a simple apparatus which will give the same appearance to the wood and can be controlled with ease. Fuming wood is one of those interesting processes by which wood is given the characteristic appearance of antiquity, and it is particularly useful for imitation period carvings.

There are several different kinds of oak, and each of them calls for a slight variation of treatment during fuming. For this reason the different species should not be mixed during fuming. It is a matter of knowing how long each type will take to darken.

One advantage of fuming is that you do not apply any fluid to the wood, but the surface must be absolutely free from grease and other substances, because this creates patchiness.

The fuming chamber can be of any size, depending on the dimensions of the pieces you want to treat. The primary need is that it is absolutely airtight. One way of doing this cheaply is to take a cardboard carton and cover it with adhesive-backed plastic sheeting, ensuring that all the joints are sealed up. A door of sufficient size to admit carvings should be cut, and they should be placed in such a way as to allow the fumes to circulate freely over all the surfaces to be fumed.

In the side of the container make a small hole to admit a testing stick of the same wood as the carving. Make sure that it is an airtight fit with a sizeable area of the stick inside the cabinet. This enables you to take test readings during fuming without disturbing the carving within.

The liquid used for fuming is 0·880 ammonia, freely obtainable from hardware stores. Depending on the size of the cabinet, two or more saucers or shallow containers are placed inside. The carving should already be in position.

The degree of darkening should be checked daily, or twice daily, depending on the concentration of fumes.

There are various tricks of the trade connected with oak and chestnut fuming. The process can be speeded up if you coat the carving with a solution made by dissolving 1 oz of tannin powder in 1 qt of water. If you want a red hue to show in the fumed carving, coat the carving with a solution made by dissolving $\frac{3}{4}$ oz pyrogallic acid in 1 qt of water.

Fumed oak or chestnut can be finished with a wax polish or by oiling with boiled linseed oil. Occasionally, a French polish is used, but this gives a somewhat hard appearance. If oil is used, then it should be in a percentage of 1 of oil to 3 of turpentine, or turpentine substitute. It can be used quite liberally if it is well rubbed in, and any surplus should be removed before the carving is allowed to dry. Beeswax dissolved in turpentine is the best wax polish. If a truly antique appearance is required, a small quantity of lampblack can be added before the final waxing.

An alternative finish for fumed oak is by burnishing. By this means the polish is on the surface of the wood itself and the sheen of wax polish is put on top of it. The burnisher can be a piece of wood of the same species or the handle of one of those old-fashioned toothbrushes – but not plastic, which is too soft for the job. If it is correctly done, any minute scratches will disappear and a perfectly smooth surface result. One thing to remember is that the burnishing tool must run with the grain, never across it. Once the sheen appears, polish should be applied sparingly.

Makers of 'antique' furniture as distinct from 'reproduction' use a variety of methods to age oak, including the use of files, rasps and even chains, which are brought down with force across edges and surfaces to suggest the marks of age.

Central European fakers use two methods of 'antiquing' carvings, rubbed and reproduction. In the rubbed method the raised sections of the carving are stained less and left lighter. During the staining Vandyke crystals are used in solution, and the carving is then coated and afterwards wiped with a clean cloth while the surface is still wet. The effect is that the deeper cut sections absorb the stain, and the higher ones, which are wiped, remain lighter. If too much stain is left on the high surfaces, fine glasspaper can be used to lighten it. Wax polish is used for final finishing.

Another finish with a quick action is to use Vandyke crystals with a very small quantity of ammonia, which helps it to penetrate deeply into the grain and bring out the figuring. A modified method is to use walnut oil stain or mix it with mahogany stain. Leave for a day to dry out, then rub it over with pumice powder on a cloth. This will lighten the colour. Finish with wax polish mixed with lampblack. Depending on how liberal you are with the wax, it will become impacted in cracks and crevices.

One of the best ways of making oak carvings look antique is by pickling, and it is done in the following way. A quantity of unslaked lime is put in a bucket. When it has cooled off, the white lime will form a residue. Pour the water into another bucket and to it add two pints of water, $\frac{1}{4}$ lb of caustic soda, 3 more pints of water and $\frac{3}{4}$ of a cupful of chloride of lime. If a darker shade is required, $\frac{1}{2}$ a cup of ammonia can be added. The carving is placed in this solution for as long as it takes to affect the wood. Frequent inspection is recommended. When the required stage is reached, the carving is put through three clean-water washes. The colour will be a lasting brown which can be increased by the application of bichromate of potash. When the wood has dried out, polish with a wax containing lampblack.

One last method of giving a weathered finish to oak or chestnut. Sandpaper it down and dust the surface, then sponge to raise any loose fibres. Dissolve 1 oz of oak stain crystals in 1 qt of water, and brush into the grain with a semi-stiff brush. Seal in the stain with a thin orange shellac. When it is completely dry, sandpaper down the surface and apply another four coats of the same shellac, rubbing down with sandpaper as each coat dries. The last coat should be rubbed down with pumice stone and linseed oil, mixed into a paste.

Let me stress that the foregoing is not meant to advocate fakery or even open copying. But the craftsman experimenting freely should have a wide range of effects at his disposal.

A note on Shellac

Shellac has been used for centuries, and the wood carver need not spurn it, for it seals the wood and at the same time enhances the figuring. You have only to look at furniture made in the seventeenth century to see the finish which is possible.

The lac bug, found in India and Ceylon, exudes a tough material which becomes its shroud. An infested bush or tree can become completely encrusted by the time the millions of dead bugs are harvested. After crushing, the material is melted down and stretched in sheets, then broken into flakes.

In preparation the flaked shellac is dissolved in denatured alcohol and then bottled. There are different grades of shellac, referred to by dealers as 5, 4 and 3 lb shellac. This refers to the amount of flake dissolved in one gallon of alcohol. The carver can, of course, dilute shellac to any consistency, bearing in mind that the thinner the fluid, the easier it is to apply. Thick shellac is difficult to apply, because it drags the brush and often leaves marks which are hard to remove. It is far better to apply about five coats of thin shellac than one thick one, which may remain tacky for several weeks.

Shellac is either white or orange coloured. Natural shellac is orange and this hue will show up, especially if the wood is bleached beforehand. It can be used quite safely on darker woods, such as oak, mahogany or walnut, but for lighter woods white shellac, which is actually eggshell in colour, is more suitable. The wood must be absolutely dry before it is applied, otherwise you get a cloudy effect.

Shellac is a very versatile material, and it may be used as a base or sealing material. If used as a base, it will provide a good grounding for almost any other type of finish. To create a good finish, shellac should be applied in several coats with a good sandpapering down between coats. It is put on with a brush and you have to operate quickly, working along the grain, not against it. Depending on the size and area, it is a good idea to work outwards from the centre, and the coats can be applied at three-hour intervals, but the previous coat must be absolutely dry before proceeding.

Although it offers many other advantages, shellac is not waterproof and contact with moisture turns it white. Heat will blister or crack it, and any contact with alcohol will, of course, dissolve it.

Shellac is the basis of French polish, which originated in the seventeenth century, consisting of a gradual build-up of shellac, using a soft pad for application. The best is a 5 lb shellac, which has plenty of body and enables you to cut it down by dilution if necessary.

Staining – Oil based

The judicious application of stain will enhance many a carving, especially where lighter woods are concerned, because many of them look a little anaemic unless they are toned down. The easiest stain to obtain is oil-based and it is penetrating. The action of one stain on any particular wood is not the same as on all woods, and for this reason manufacturers have created a very wide range, almost one for each type of wood. Here is a selection:

Shade	Reaction colour if used on same wood
Fumed Oak	Dark brown
Golden Oak	Light brown
Light Oak	Yellow
English Brown	Dark brown
Brown Mahogany	Red-brown
Red Mahogany	Deep brown
Golden Maple	Yellow
Red Maple	Red
Light Maple	White
American Walnut	Dark brown
French Walnut	Light brown

An obvious advantage of using the penetrating oil-based stain is that it immediately shows up the figuring, but it takes more than twenty-four hours to dry, and you cannot use a paste filler, because it just will not take. A wash of shellac is the best finish.

Oil stain is applied after the wood has been thoroughly cleaned, and a softish brush is recommended. The stain should be applied with the grain, never against it.

Staining – Water-based

A great many wood carvers use water stain in preference to oil stain because it takes quickly to the wood and gives a clearer finish. This is, of course, a matter of opinion. Chemically speaking, water stain contains coal tar and vegetable dye. The main advantage is the wide range of hues available, and you can dilute each of them for delicate hues if needed. Making the stains by mixing powder colour (see below) is quite simple, although you should start with a light shade, adding more powder until the required depth is reached. Some beginners make the mistake of dumping all the powder in the water, and this can create a muddy-looking solution.

To prepare the stain use 1 oz of powder to a quart of water. Boil the water, remove from the stove and pour into a metal can, then gradually stir in the powder. As remarked above, the actual shade can be varied by reducing or increasing the amount of powder.

Perhaps the only disadvantage of water stain is that it raises the wood fibres, but this can be defeated by first of all applying a coat of perfectly clean water to the carving, and when it is dry the surface can be sandpapered down with medium and fine sandpapers. Thus, when the stain is applied, the grain is not affected.

The stain should be put on with a fairly stiff brush to help it into the wood pores, and brushing should be rapid to avoid uneven areas. The brush should be fully charged at each brushing, and you will find that it is rapidly absorbed, so a plentiful supply of stain should be kept in hand.

Various home-made and improvised stains

Vinegar. If you pour a pint of white vinegar over some ordinary nails and leave it for about eight hours, then filter the liquid through a fine muslin to remove any bits, you will create an excellent stain for colouring pine and similar woods to an antique grey. This is much used by art forgers of 'antique' carvings on the Continent.

Permanganate of Potash. Dissolve 2 oz of crystals in a quart of water. This gives a substantial fluid for staining wood brown, and it is particularly useful for the lighter woods.

Ammonia. Use a twenty-six per cent ammonia and mix with water until it causes oak to darken. This is a variation of fuming, but is only suitable for temporary effects.

Fillers

Many carvers wish to create a perfectly smooth finish, and this is done by filling the pores. There are two types of filler – a paste for open-grained wood, and a liquid for close-grained woods. The necessary quality is that the filler shall stick to the wood without any shrinkage or crumbling. Natural wood filler is made from quartz powder, linseed oil, japan drier and boiled linseed oil. Nowadays fillers to match any wood colour can be purchased.

Paste filler is best for the following woods:

	Ash	Oak	Chestnut	Elm

In use it should be thinned down with benzine until it is creamy, then brushed on a section at a time, both with and across the grain. Now make a hessian pad and rub down the surface, working across the grain to avoid removing the filled sections, many of which are almost microscopic. Take a clean linen cloth and wipe away any surplus filler, still working across the grain.

Liquid filler is used on the following woods:

Bass	Beech	Cherry	Gum	Poplar	Birch
Cedar	Fir	Pine	Spruce		

It is brushed on and then wiped to prevent residue from accumulating.

Shellac or varnish are quite adequate as fillers for close-grained woods, and shellac is best used in a fifty/fifty mixture with alcohol, and it can be applied in long, even strokes with sandpapering between each of three coats. Varnish will take longer to dry and harden, and it should not be used if you intend finishing with lacquer.

133

Bleaching

This method enables you to lighten wood and then finish it to any desired colour. You can also use it to remove an existing colour of a carving and then re-finish it in a better way. Most carvers adapt hydrogen peroxide in a concentrated 30 per cent solution in the following way:

Four oz lye are dissolved in 1 qt of water, and while this is still hot it is dabbed on to the area to be bleached. Note: it should not come in contact with the skin.

As soon as the area is dry, hydrogen peroxide should be dabbed on. The bleaching will commence immediately, and when it is finished the carving should be held under the tap to wash away all traces of lye and hydrogen peroxide.

For bleaching pine and maple and other light woods the use of oxalic acid and hypo is recommended. Between 1 and 4 oz oxalic acid (depending on the strength required) are dissolved in a quart of hot water. Hypo (the photographic chemical) is dissolved in a ratio of 2 to 4 oz to a quart of water. The oxalic acid is applied to the wood with a cloth dabber and allowed to dry, then the hypo solution is put on with another cloth. Do not use the same cloth for each dabbing. After ten to fifteen minutes the surface can be washed in a solution made by dissolving 1 oz borax in 1 qt of water.

White pine is bleached with laundry bleach, but it is so mild that in the ratio of ½ pt to 1 gal. of water the lightening of the wood will be very gradual. A thorough washing in running water should be given. When the bleached area has dried, it should be smoothed with sandpaper.

Blond finishes

Nowadays many wood carvers are going over to the old idea of leaving a carving unstained but with a final polish. This has the advantage of enhancing line in dimensional carvings, and it may apply to parts of some relief carvings.

Basically, the blond finish is achieved by bleaching, as described above, and if a carving can be totally submerged in the bleach, all the better. Then dry.

A white lacquer is now applied so as to seal the surface, and a clear-gloss lacquer is put on. A second coat should be given about twenty-four hours later, then rubbed down with very fine steel wool or a paste made from a mixture of linseed oil and pumice powder. To finish, polish with beeswax and turpentine.

The foregoing applies to close-grained woods. The following can be used for open-grained woods, such as walnut, oak and mahogany.

Use the same process as with close-grained wood up to the sandpapering after the bleaching. Now use a neutral filler paste to fill the wood pores. It should set in between five and ten minutes and the surplus should be wiped away in the meantime. After twenty-four hours apply one coat of white shellac, and sandpaper when dry. Then apply a finishing coat of shellac, lacquer or good varnish. Rub down with fine steel wool. Apply a second coat, followed by wax polish.

Gold finish

Many carvings can be enriched by a good gold finish, but this should not be overdone, because not all carvings are improved by gilding. Assuming that you are starting with a newly carved piece, it should be thoroughly cleaned and sandpapered, and a coat of shellac applied. As soon as the shellac is dry paint it over again with shellac to which a spot of tube red has been added. Note: do not overdo the red tint. It is there merely to give body to the gold. When it is dry, sandpaper. Finally, paint over with any good standard gold bronze.

134

Any paint dealer will supply ready-mixed gold bronze. Care should be taken to ensure an even coat while brushing. To finish, use orange shellac.

For gilding in the traditional style, here is the method:

Two coats of white lead and oil paint are applied to the carving. It should take four to five days to harden. Now coat with French gold size and wait until it becomes tacky. It should not be allowed to dry out completely.

The gold leaf is supplied in 'books', and it comes as board or mounted leaf. Gold supplied as mounted leaf sticks to a tissue material, whereas board leaf has no tissue. The thickness is about two ten-thousandths of an inch. When you use it, you must lift it from the book to the carving, avoiding any wrinkling or folding. This is done by lifting the leaf itself with a one-inch squirrel hair brush, but first prepare the brush by passing it across velvet to charge it with static electricity. Take the brush to the sheet of gold and place it against the edge, making a very slight twisting motion. The gold will lift and it can be placed in position on the tacky surface of the carving. When it is in position, it cannot be shifted. Any uncovered surfaces can be filled in with slivers of gold. It will be found that if overlaps do happen to occur, the gold will crumble, and this crumbled gold can also be used to fill in any bare areas.

About one week after the gold has been applied, the size should be firm enough for final treatment. The best quality cotton wool or fine silk velvet is used to stroke it flat and firm. This will also serve to polish the gold to a lasting finish.

Polychromy

Many carved statues in ancient times were painted to give a lifelike appearance to features, robes and decoration, and this sprang from the habit of primitive races of using colours taken from the earth and plants. Red and black were the primary colours with yellow, white, blue and green. Colour was often smeared on in a flat coating with little attempt at artistry. Polychromy, or painting, was practised by the ancient Egyptians, but they used brushes for finer detail. The Greeks painted statuary, notably in the huge chryselephantine statues by Phidias. Later the Romans painted their statuary, as did Gothic sculptors, and the practice continued up to the Renaissance.

The long tradition of polychromy has been broken by the modern trend in leaving carvings unpainted. But for the carver who wishes to experiment, here is the method:

Tube colour is used and there is, of course, no limit to the number of coats which can be applied. The surface should be prepared with two coats of white paint to seal the grain. A white lead base is best for the undercoating together with linseed oil and turpentine mixed together.

Providing the painting is well done and not garish, there is no reason why it should not enhance a carving, and examples of it can be seen in Plates 71A and B, where polychroming has brought to life the usually static civic symbols.

Gesso

The word itself comes from the Italian and the Latin (*gypsum*) for plaster of Paris, the more specifically when it is used as a ground for painting. Nowadays it is also used as a base for gilding. Because of its nature, it covers the wood completely with a smooth finish.

The primary ingredient of gesso is plaster of Paris or a mixture of whiting size, the latter being made from gelatine. The best way of slaking the plaster of Paris is by keeping it in a bucket for four or five weeks. The water will be absorbed and a daily renewal may be necessary.

The size is made by adding 1 oz of edible gelatine to 16 oz of water and heating in a double saucepan, simmering until it grows firm. Reheat and melt, then stir into the plaster of Paris. The stuff is put on with a soft brush, allowed to dry, and a fine sandpaper is used to rub it down. Brush on a second coat and smooth down while wet, using the palm of the hand. A third coat should prove sufficient, and painting or gilding can follow.

71 *Two fine examples of traditional civic carving by Messrs Green and Vardy, now known as Heal Furniture Limited. Both are polychromed. 'A' is the coat of arms of the County of Berkshire, and is one of a pair mounted on Newbury Court House. 'B' is the coat of arms of Chesterton Rural District Council. Photographs by courtesy of Heal Furniture Limited.*

A

NIET · ZONDER · ARBYT

B

A basic finishing kit for wood carvers

Top Surface Finishers

White shellac
Orange shellac
Varnish (flat)
Lacquer (clear)
Lacquer (sealer)

Solvents

Turpentine or turpentine substitute
Alcohol (denatured)
Lacquer (thinners)

Oils

Boiled linseed oil
Raw linseed oil

Dry Powder Colours

Raw Umber
Burnt Umber
Red Vermilion
Zinc White
Black
French Ochre
Vandyke Brown

Water Soluble Colours

Walnut
Red Mahogany
Brown Mahogany
Brown
Dark Oak
Light Oak
Silver Grey
Black (Nigrosene)

Rubbing Materials

No. 2/0 steel wool
No. 2/0 pumice powder
Garnet cloth (all grades)
Sandpaper (all grades)
Cheesecloth or lint-free rags

Brushes

A selection of soft to medium bristle of various sizes.

A note of caution

Carvers use large quantities of rags when applying polishes containing oil
and shellac. A rubber which becomes hard and crusty should be thrown
away, because it will scratch the surface and do damage which is hard
to remove. But this is not the main reason for throwing away oil-soaked and
other rags. The reason is FIRE! Some finishing fluids when mixed up and
crushed together are quite capable of spontaneous combustion, and if you
finish working late at night, leaving rags all over the bench, you may wake
up to find your house or workshop on fire. Nor is it a good idea to jam

unwanted rags together into a bin, because this incurs a fire risk. The best idea is to have a bucket of water near your bench, and into it toss rags as soon as you finish with them. The resultant appearance of the bucket may not be pretty to look at, and it will smell even worse, but it will save you from premature cremation.

THE FINISHING OF WOOD THROUGH THE AGES

JACOBEAN 1603–49 CROMWELLIAN 1649–60	Some finished with wax or oil, often with gum copal varnish. Some black and gilded. Poppy oil was the basis of many finishes with a coating of wax made by dissolving it in turpentine and making up into paste.
WILLIAM AND MARY 1688–1702	Oil finish as a rule but there was a preponderance of painted carving with some gilding on black, scarlet or blue. Walnut carving was left unfinished. A turpentine and wax polish was often used.
QUEEN ANNE 1702–14 EARLY GEORGIAN 1714–60	Oil and wax polishes were used, but often white painted. A great deal of mahogany and walnut carving appeared, some of it lacquered. Oak was the favourite carving wood with an oil and wax finish. Shellac was used plentifully.
LOUIS XIV 1643–1715 LOUIS XV 1715–74	The carving of soft wood was finished with lacquer, and much carving was enhanced with metal inlay and the use of tortoiseshell.
CHIPPENDALE 1705–79	A certain amount of lacquering, but most carving was finished with oil and turpentine polish.
ADAM BROTHERS 1762–90	A flowering of exquisite and extravagant carving with floriation in abundance and some Greek motifs. Finishing with oil and turpentine.
HEPPLEWHITE d. 1786	Inlays with little carving, but a great deal of gilding. Oil and wax finishing.
LOUIS XVI 1774–93	The introduction of French polish.
SHERATON 1750–1806	The introduction of a refined form of oil and wax polishing.
EMPIRE 1793–1830	Some gilding. Some varnishing with a finish of French polish and some red staining with water-soluble colours. Fumed oak introduced.
AMERICAN EMPIRE 1793–1830	French polish, water-soluble stains and some painting. Wax polishes.

139

72

74A

IN MEMORY
OF THOSE OF
NEW ALRESFOR
WHO GAVE THE
LIVES IN THE WA

74B

74C

72 'Figure' by Harry Maddocks. 7½ in. high. Mahogany. There is something spectral about this figure, emphasized by the shape of the head. Maddocks is a South Wales schoolmaster and a former Chief Mate in the Merchant Service. He is self-taught. Author's collection. Photograph by Derek Gabriel.

73 Carving in the drawing room of the Bull Inn, Long Melford, Suffolk. There is something vaguely humorous about the six faces, and the execution is amateurish but effective. Photograph by courtesy of the British Travel Association.

74 English wood carvers of the present day at work.
A and B Eric Sharp of Martyr Worthy, Wiltshire, lettering a war memorial plaque.
C Figure carving at Bridgeman and Son Limited.
D R. Gill of Norwood, Yorkshire, carving a rebus.
E R. Wilkinson of Brampton-on-Morthen carving a bracket.

74D

73

74E

141

F R. Thompson of Thirsk, Yorkshire, carving an organ screen.
G Carving a coat of arms at L'etacq Woodcraft.
H A carved butter mould from Howard Brothers, Chesham, Bucks.
I A spoon and ladle carved by Ienan Evans of Y Glyn Tregrod, Cardiganshire.
Acknowledgements: A–G by courtesy of Rural Industries Bureau; H and I by courtesy of the British Travel Association.

75 Symbolic wood sculpture from Australia. Bunbulame, the rain goddess. The rectangle of dots on the body represents the clouds, and the vertical bands suggest rain. The goddess is powerful in Arnhem Land. Photograph by courtesy of the Australian News and Information Bureau.

74F

74G

142

74H

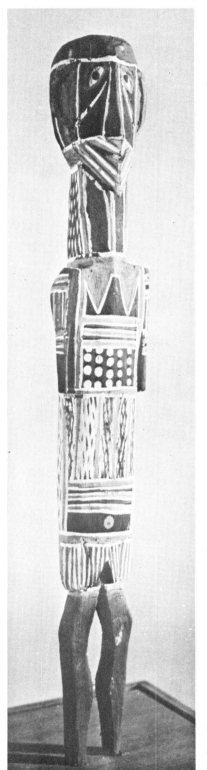

75

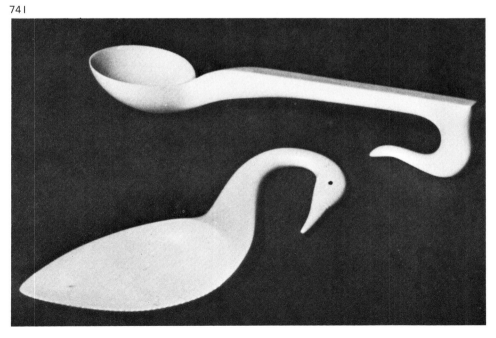

74I

143

76 Angers, France, Maison d'Adam,
date unknown. A delightfully human
study which forms part of a pillar.
Photograph: Boudot-Lamotte by
courtesy of the French Government
Tourist Office.

77 Thiers, France, 'The House of the
Wooden Man'. A curious piece of
carving. Photograph by courtesy of the
French Government Tourist Office.

78 The work of Nancy Catford, an
English carver.
A Limewood to a design by
J. Rodney Stone for Messrs Spillers
Limited.

A

144

B

C

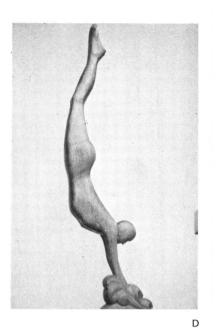

D

E

B   Mahogany. 'Tennis Player'. 60 in. high. For Messrs Spillers Limited.
C   Oak, 'Washing Cat'. 10 in.
D   Honduras Mahogany. 'Diver'. 66 in. high. For Messrs Spillers Limited.
E   Mahogany. 'Heron'. 16 in.×5 in.×3 in. Photographs by courtesy of Miss Nancy Catford.

145

146

79, 80 *'The Fairies' Tree' in Fitzroy Gardens, Melbourne, Australia, was carved by Ola Cohn as a gift to the children of the city. It occupied three years in the early 'thirties. Miss Cohn died in 1964. Photographs by courtesy of the Australian News and Information Bureau.*

81 'Shovelling Movement' by
Gerald Lewers, an Australian carver
who also works in stone. Mulberry.
Photographed by Cliff Bottomley by
courtesy of the Australian News and
Information Bureau.

82 *'Native Head' by Clifford Last, who has worked in many Australian timbers. Ironbark. Photographed by Jack Gallagher by courtesy of the Australian News and Information Bureau.*

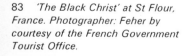

83　'The Black Christ' at St Flour,
France. Photographer: Feher by
courtesy of the French Government
Tourist Office.

84　'Crucifixion' by the English wood
sculptor, Robert W. Forsyth, for the
Chapel of Our Lady of Pity, Dover.
14 ft 6 in.×6 ft. Photographs by
courtesy of Aaron Hildick Limited,
Sheffield.

A

B

152

C

D

85 The Cunard line patronized wood carvers and sculptors for the interior decoration of the Queen Mary and Queen Elizabeth. These photographs are representative of the styles of various craftsmen-artists. Photographs by courtesy of the Cunard Line Limited.
A 'Wood' by Norman Forrest was one of a series of nine bas reliefs in the Cabin Class Smoking Room. Each relief represents a material used in the construction of the ship.
B Wood sculpture in a First Class stateroom. Sculptor unknown.
C This relief by Bainbridge Copnall for the Queen Mary shows the Great Eastern (1860), Mauretania (1907) and Queen Mary (1936). It was positioned in the Main Restaurant.
D Three groups from the former Long Gallery of the Queen Mary carved in lime by Bainbridge Copnall.

E

F

E   *Carved and pierced panels by
James Woodford depicting shipboard
activities aboard* Queen Mary *in the
First Class Smoking Room. Lime*
F   *Carved and pierced panel by
James Woodford depicting sporting
activities aboard* Queen Mary *in the
First Class Smoking Room. Lime.*

154

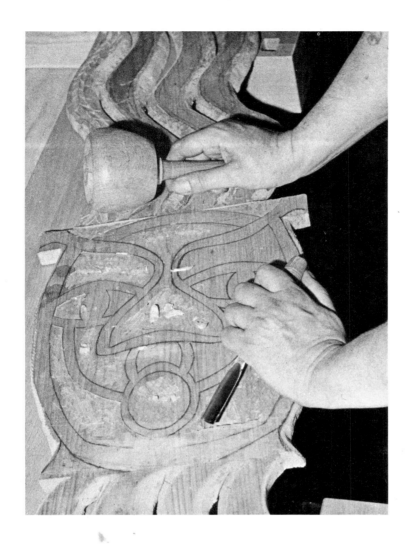

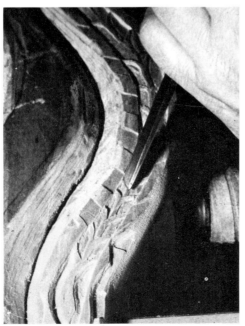

86 *Beginning to carve a primitive 4 ft 6 in. mask from a pine plank. One feature of the face is that it has no straight lines, and the pierced wood is all cut at an angle. The eight 'horns' at top and bottom are in process of being chip carved, using the straight chisel. The preliminary work on the face was done with the broadest gouge. Photograph by Derek Gabriel.*

11

Wood Carvers of the Present Day

87A *John Skelton working on*
'Rhythmic Form'.
87B, C, D, E   *Also by John Skelton,*
see pages 158–162

This is by no means comprehensive, but it is included to give the reader names to look out for in galleries and collections. Photographs of the work of these wood carvers and sculptors can be found in the majority of pictorial books on modern art, also in the catalogues of galleries. The student is urged to study them.

Adams, Robert. b. 1917, Northampton. Studied Northampton School of Art. First exhibition 1947. Represented at São Paulo Biennials, 1951 and 1957, and open-air exhibitions at Middleheim, 1953, and London, 1954 and 1957. Instructor at London School of Arts and Crafts since 1949. Has also worked in metal, concrete and stone.

Barlach, Ernst. (1870–1938) b. Wedel, Holstein. d. Rostock. Studied at School of Arts and Crafts, Hamburg, then Dresden Academy. Principal work in wood is 'Frieze of Listeners', a screen of nine oak figures as a commemorative monument to Beethoven in the church of St Catherine, Lübeck. Three panels were completed, and the carving is in the Gothic style.

Baum, Otto. b. 1900, Leonberg, Württemberg. First studied engineering, then served in the navy, 1914–18. Between 1924–7 and 1931–3 studied at Stuttgart Academy under Spiegel and Waldschmidt. Noted for reliefs in wood which have subjects barely raised.

Belling, Rudolf. b. 1886, Berlin. Pupil of Peter Bruer. Founded November-gruppe 1918. As a result of Hitler regime fled to Turkey where he now teaches sculpture. Works mainly in the abstract and was a forerunner of Henry Moore in typical forms with spatial values.

Beothy, Etienne. b. 1897, Heves, Hungary. Studied at School of Architecture, Budapest. Left architecture 1920 to become a sculptor, and lived in Paris. Earliest works executed mainly in wood with calculated proportions. His starting point was the human form. 'The Sea. Opus 67 Mobile' in Brazilian rosewood, now in the Adler Collection, Geneva, typifies the main body of his work.

Bertoni, Wander. b. 1925, Codisotto, Italy. Now lives in Vienna. Studied at the Viennese Art Academy. His most interesting work in polychromed wood is 'Imaginary Alphabet', a representation of the sounds of letters.

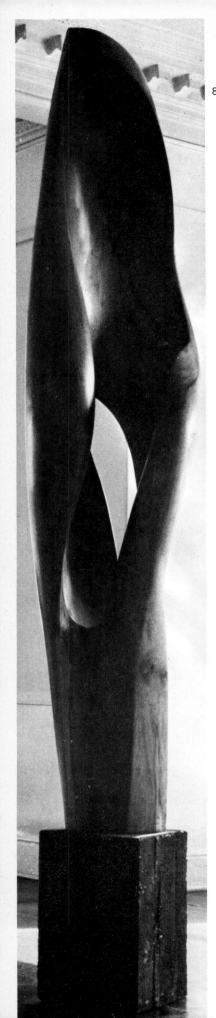

87B

Bourgeois, Louise. b. 1911, Paris. Studied at the Lycée Fénelon and the Sorbonne, and has worked in New York since 1938. First exhibition at the Berk Schaefer Gallery, New York. Her main theme is an attempt to link tension and repose in a series of elongated wood forms which are neither abstract nor symbolic but rise from the ground.

Brancusi, Constantin. (1876–1957) b. Targu Jin, Rumania, and died in Paris. Started life as an apprentice cabinet maker and was awarded scholarship to Bucharest, 1898, studying sculpture and architecture. Went to Paris after working in Munich, Zurich and Basle. Between 1914–18 sculpted in wood, including 'Prodigal Son', 'Caryatid' and 'Chimera', using oak. Some of his work shows African influences but is also humorous. His later wood sculpture explored the abstract in the form of 'Eve' (1921), 'The Chieftain' (1922), 'Socrates' (1923) and 'Endless Column', 98 ft high. This was later cast in steel and gilded, and now stands in his birthplace at the foot of the Carpathian Mountains.

Brignoni, Serge. b. 1903, Chiasso, Switzerland. Experimented in wood sculpture from 1932, making imaginary animal and vegetable hybrids, and creating monstrous plant forms. Lives in Berne and in 1956 was represented at the Venice and São Paulo Biennials.

Calo, Aldo. b. 1910, San Cesario di Lecce, Italy. Studied at Lecce Art School and the Institute of Art, Florence. First exhibition 1947 at Cavallino Gallery, Venice. Director of the Institute of Art, Volterra, and is now in charge of the Institute of Rome. In 'Biform' he mixes two media, wood and iron, to contrast materials and styles.

Cantre, Joseph. (1890–1957) b. Ghent, Belgium. Was book illustrator, wood engraver and designer, but turned to wood sculpture. Early commissions were for decorative sculpture in churches at Heeswijck and Hilversum, and later a figure for the tomb of Rene de Clercq at Lage Vuurse, Holland, also a monument to Edouard Anseele, Ghent.

Cardenas, Augustin. b. 1927, Matanzas, Cuba. In 1954 received the National Prize for Sculpture of Cuba. Went to Paris in 1955. Worked originally in plaster, then wood in tall vertical columns under the general title, 'Totems'.

Castelli, Alfio. b. 1917, Senigallia, Italy. Studied at Florence Academy and the Academy of Rome. First one-man show, Rome, 1940. His recent carving has been in bas-relief and all small in size.

Colvin, Marta. b. 1917, Chillan, Chile. Studied at Santiago Academy, and went to Paris in 1948 on scholarship. Exhibitions at various South American centres, including Lima, Rio de Janeiro. Her carvings are a synthesis of something between plant and human forms. Taught sculpture at Santiago Academy, and is influenced by pre-Columbian and Pacific art.

Condoy, Honorio Garcia. (1900–53) b. Saragossa, Spain. Held first one-man show when he was eighteen, and went to Paris in 1929. The hallmark of much of his post-Cubist work is an attempt at dissolving away the individuality of the model.

87C

87B   *'Rhythmic Form' – completed Towner Art Gallery, Eastbourne.*
C   *Miraculum Creations completed for United Art Pavilion, Yugoslavia. Oak, Stainless Steel and Copper. 9 ft high.*

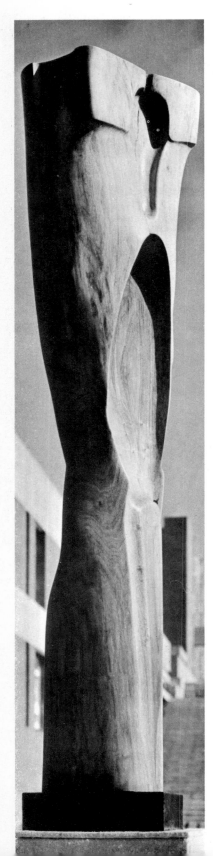

D *Torso of Adam. Walnut. 4 ft 9 in. high (Photo: John Carter)*

Dodeigne, Eugene. b. 1923, Rouvreux, near Liège. Studied at the Ecole des Beaux-Arts, Tourcoing, and Académie des Beaux Arts, Paris. One-man exhibitions at Tourcoing and the Galerie Claude Bernard, Paris. Was trained in stone carving, but worked in wood, creating stretched figures in the Surrealist manner with a full utilization of the material.

Etienne-Martin. b. 1913, Loriol (Drons), France. Joined the Ecole des Beaux-Arts, Lyons, at 16. Has experimented widely with wood and string sculptures.

Fazzini, Pericle. b. 1913, Grottamare, Italy. Worked with his father as a cabinet maker, then studied sculpture in Rome, 1929. 'The Dance', 1934, was a large carving which attracted attention. Won sculpture prize, Venice Biennale, 1954. Later works in wood included 'Portrait of Colonel Paiizzi', 1943.

Gauguin, Paul. (1848–1903) b. Paris, died at Atuana, Marquesas Islands. Influenced by the Impressionists, he left a business career, and painted in Paris, Brittany and Martinique. When in Tahiti he started wood carving, decorating his own hut with adaptations of native art. In Brittany he carved furniture, clogs and walking sticks.

Gili, Marcel. b. 1914, Thuir, France. Main work in terracotta, but some wood sculpture, including 'The Technician', 9 ft high.

Hartung, Karl. b. 1908, Hamburg, and studied at Hamburg School of Arts and Crafts. At the age of 21 went to Paris, then Florence, Hamburg and Berlin. Influenced by the abstract.

Hepworth, Barbara. b. 1903, Wakefield, Yorkshire. Studied at Leeds School of Art and Royal College of Art. Spent three years in Italy on travelling scholarship. First exhibition 1928, London, and many international exhibitions, including open-air shows in London, 1949–57. Her work is characterized by a reaction to her materials, which include metal, stone and wood, the latter exemplified in her 1955 work, 'Two Figures, Menhirs', done in teak. Some open and hollow forms are string threaded, often with concave surfaces painted white.

Hoflehner, Rudolf. b. 1916, Linz, Austria. Learned techniques with materials while at engineering school, and taught at Linz School of Arts and Crafts. In 1951 became independent and settled in Vienna. Represented in 1954 and 1956 at the Venice Biennale. Self-taught, he started with wood carving and sculpture, but later passed on to metal working.

Kohn, Gabriel. b. 1910, Philadelphia. Son of an engraver. Studied at the Cooper Union with Gaetano Cecere, later in New York. Hon. Mention for monument in 'The Unknown Political Prisoner' competition. Created his own style in wood, geometric and irregular shapes, using laminated woods with machined and perfectly smooth finishes.

Kozaric, Ivan. b. 1921, Petrinja, Yugoslavia. Trained at Zagreb Academy. Created 'The Stations of the Cross' for the church at Senj, also a sporting subject now in Zagreb. Represented in 1960 at the Salon de la Jeune Sculpture.

Latorre, Jacinto. b. 1905, Irun, Spain. Almost completely self-taught, but later had some training at the Académie de la Grande-Chaumière for three years. In 1952 won a prize in 'The Unknown Political Prisoner' competition. Apart from wood, also works in iron, bronze and copper.

Lipton, Seymour. b. 1903, New York. Received degree in dentistry at Columbia University. From 1935–45 produced a large number of figurative carvings in wood, but now works in metals.

Martinez, Richier. b. 1928, San Pedro de Macaris, Dominican Republic. Awarded a sculpture prize at school and in 1946 was appointed art teacher. Went to Bueños Aires Art School 1950, left in 1952 and settled in Paris. Exhibited at Salon d'Art Libre, Salon de Mai and Salon d'Automne. His work is marked by a purity but contains overtones of the Caribbean.

E *Torso of Woman. Yew. 3 ft high. (Photo: University of Sussex Library)*

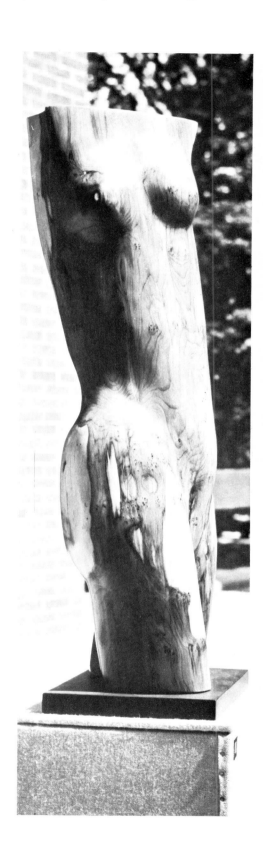

Matare, Ewald. b. 1887, Aix-la-Chapelle. Left painting for sculpture in 1920, and taught at Düsseldorf Academy. In 1953 a retrospective exhibition of his work was held at the Museum of Arts and Crafts, Hamburg. Won gold medal of Mainz Triennial, 1954. Specialized in stylized wood carvings of animals in repose. Also carved on commission many small objects such as door handles, chalices and church doors.

Moore, Henry. b. 1898, Castleford, Yorkshire, England. Trained as a teacher, but on leaving the army in 1919 went to Leeds School of Art, then Royal College of Art until 1925. First exhibition London 1928. Taught at the Royal College of Art and Chelsea School of Art. Many themes show in his work, including mother and child, family group, stricken warrior and reclining figure, and abstracts.

F   *William Shakespeare's Coat of Arms. Cedar of Lebanon.* 3 ft *high. Shakespeare Trust Conference Room, Stratford on Avon.*

Nevelson, Louise. b. Kiev, Russia, 1900, and went to America in 1905 and studied in the Art Students' League, New York, then went to Munich. First exhibition 1940 at Nierendorf Gallery, New York. Main work all wood sculpture.

Noll, Alexandre. b. 1890, Rheims. Began carving in 1920 and made many articles of general utility. Influenced by Negro and Chinese art. First exhibition Salon d'Automne, 1921. Works in walnut, sycamore, ebony, teak and mahogany. In one period carved entire suites of furniture out of solid blocks of wood. Exhibited in 1943 at the Compagnie des Arts Français, and in 1946 at the Salon des Réalités Nouvelles.

Nuñez del Prado, Marina. b. 1912, La Paz, Bolivia. Gave up teaching at 27 and went on grant to U.S.A. Exhibitions in 1952 (Venice Biennale) and Paris (1953). Earliest works influenced by Indian culture.

Pan Marta. b. 1923, Budapest. Studied in her native city and went to Paris in 1947. Participated in Salon des Réalités Nouvelles since 1950 and in exhibitions at Nantes and Amsterdam. Two of her woodcarvings formed part of the decor in ballets produced by Maurice Béjart.

Phillips, Helen. b. 1913, Fresno, California. Trained at Art School of California, and went to Paris and London, being represented at the Salon de la Jeune Sculpture and Salon de Mai. Has developed a non-figurative style, and worked in clay, plaster, stone and wood.

Roussil, Robert. b. 1925, Montreal, Canada. Trained at Montreal Art Association. Principal work, 'Human Galaxy', 36 ft high for a public square in Montreal. Lives in South of France and holds one-man roadside exhibitions.

Skelton, John. Nephew of Eric Gill. Born in 1923, he studied at Coventry School of Art. He served in the army in India, Burma, Siam and Malaya, and five years in a stonemason's yard prior to setting up his own studio at Streat, Sussex. He believes in the value of experiment, and has worked in a variety of materials. He has twice represented Great Britain as a guest artist and sits on the Arts Council Public Sculpture Committee for Scotland. (Photographs by courtesy of John Skelton.)

88   The carving of Professor David
Pye of the Royal College of Art. These
photographs show the evolution of a
life-size figurehead for T.S.M.Y.
Brittina III, owned by Patrick Dolan. It
was carved in African Mahogany
laminated with Resorcinol
Formaldehyde glue.

A   This shows the laminated block
made of planks finishing about 2¼ in.
thick, each bandsawn to the profile of
the figure before glueing together.
The wood at each side of the head has
been sawn away, and some work done
on the sides of the block by the ship-
carpenter's adze shown in the
foreground.

B   The first stages of carving. Only
saws and an adze have been used so
far, and the adze took the carving
considerably farther just after the
photograph was taken.

C   The head before painting.

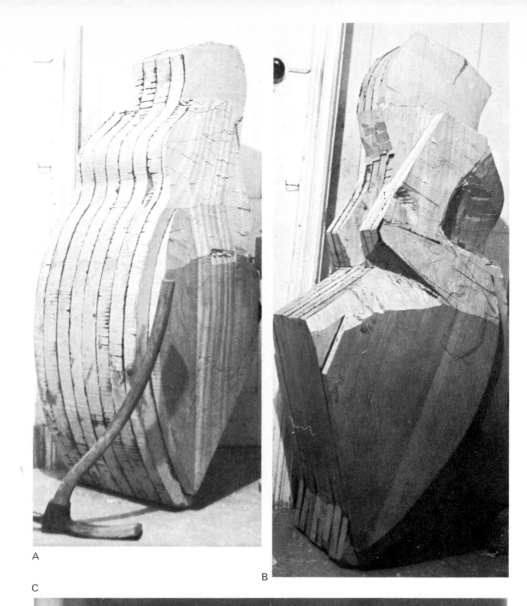

A

B

C

D

D and E *(overleaf)* *The figurehead completed and painted. (Photographs by courtesy of Professor David Pye)*

165

Stahly, François. b. 1911, Konstanz, Germany. Joined Académie Ranson in 1931, and was represented in the Salon de Mai, Salon de la Jeune Sculpture and Salon des Réalités Nouvelles. Won gold medal at Milan Triennale, 1954. First sculpture incorporated knots and curves, but later he exploited plant forms, as in 'Birth'. 'Castle of Tears' (1952) employed stalactites and cave forms.

Takis, Vassilakis. b. 1925, Athens. Self-taught, and left Greece at 29 to study in London and Paris, working first in clay, then in wood, interpreting the human form. Latterly has had exhibitions at the Salon la Jeune Sculpture and the Salon des Réalités Nouvelles.

Touret, Jean-Marie. b. 1916, Lassay, France. Trained at the Albert Magnan School, Le Mans. Several exhibitions at Galerie du Bac and Galerie Chardin, Paris. His carving is full of detail, typified in bas reliefs in designs which suggest closely-knit fences.

Underwood, Leon. b. 1890, London. Studied at Regent Street Polytechnic. Carvings made in the 'twenties show African influences. He is the author of books on primitive art. Carried out a commission for the L.C.C. monument at Hilgrove Estate, 1960.

Zadkine, Ossip. b. 1890, Smolensk, Russia. At 16 went to Sunderland, England, and studied drawing and sculpture at evening classes. Famous for his experiments in new sculptural forms from Cubist to Abstract. In 1940 evolved a system of pierced pieces to create multiple view-points. Since the war has held a number of one-man exhibitions, including Paris (1949), London (1952) and Tokyo (1954). Now teaches at the Académie de la Grande-Chaumière, Paris.

89A

89B

89 *The work of Barbara Linley-Adams, a British carver.*
A *Scops Owl. Teak.* 12 in. *high.*
B *Fawn. Western Red Cedar.* 8 in. *long.*
C *Cat. Ash.* 10 in. *high.*
D *Puma. Teak.* 18 in. *across.*

167

89C

89D

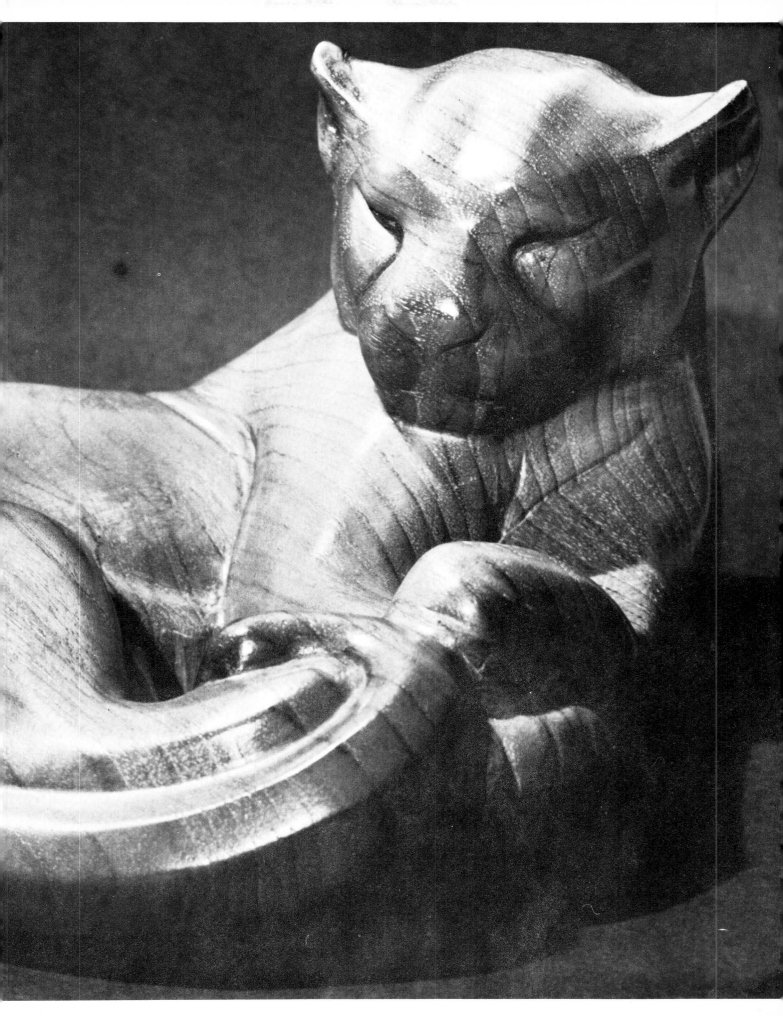

12

'I am interested in everything that does not exist, in creating something.'

Erté

A Carver's Commonplace Book

In the bottom drawer of my workbench there is an old ledger, and in it I occasionally jot down odd thoughts and ideas. This is a random selection . . .

ONE
The ultimate insult to carving – a firm of light engineers supplying hardware to cabinet makers has brought out a line of plastic reproductions made from cellulose acetate in the form of cresting, medallions and patarea. They say that by using these mockeries and sticking them on your furniture and walls and doors, a suburban house or flat can be made to look like the Palace of Versailles. They are direct copies of carvings in the Victoria and Albert Museum (surprising that the V. and A. let them in to carry out such sacrilege). They also say you cannot tell the difference between these copies and the real thing.

It seems to be just one more step in the 'getting-away-from-doing-it-yourself' trend of the times in which we are all incarcerated. It sounds terribly stuffy to decry something which will bring small but fine reproduction carvings to millions of homes, but it is much the same as the cheap reproductions of paintings and you soon see the same damned thing in every hall, lounge and lavatory. Modern man of 2000 A.D. won't know what a gouge or a chisel looks like, but he will be stuffed to capacity with reproductions of what the tools used to do. His leisure will probably be spent with play tools activated with compressed air and producing Plastic Things in a kind of government-planned domestic assembly line. Hands will atrophy through lack of use. But a few concert pianists may still be around.

TWO

I suppose it is all a matter of temperament, but carving is one of those things you can take up first thing in the morning and for which you feel an immediate interest. This emotion might not apply to people to whom everything from breathing to sleeping is hard work, and it certainly won't appeal to the growing number who cannot do anything except in a kind of mental committee. To them the workbench implies serfdom. Not long ago an acquaintance – you couldn't call him a friend – came to see me and we chatted as I went on carving. Eventually he said: 'Surely you could mechanise all that hard labour?' Sure you can. You can set yourself a production target, start an assembly line, turn out carvings by the dozen. Then you could set about finding markets for your work, open a sales office, grow ulcers and become a total idiot. Nowadays it has become hard to place an activity like wood carving and sculpture in perspective in a muddled world. The insistence on leisure and, worse, 'education for leisure', and the distinct possibility of a Ministry of Leisure, is anathema.

Many times in my own life I have had to hold down bread and butter jobs, from working in an East End pencil factory to running a mental hospital mortuary, but my mind has always been wholeheartedly on my 'outside' activities – as a rule, this has been in the writing sphere. We need to tilt the perspective and assure ourselves that what goes on in working hours simply doesn't matter a cuss. What goes on in our minds and in our hands is more important.

Industry is quite baffled by the people it employs. I heard today of a firm that is setting up an 'attitude survey' among employees to find out what the payroll people think about the company. If they do learn the truth they may be shaken.

THREE

Some of the chain stores are now selling animal carvings from Africa. Beautifully finished, like the glossy veneer they stick on bedroom suites and cocktail cabinets, they have a set and rigid plastic appearance, and they are all obviously made to a pattern devised to please the Western eye. They are quickly replacing those plaster ducks which people with no taste used to hang on the walls of their little houses. From quick inspection as I pass the counter I guess that these African imitation carvings are machine finished with power tools. There are no marks of hand tools except a little file cut here and there, and the flanks of the frozen gazelles are like mirrors. Emergent Africa, that poor savage country, is exporting her 'culture' and making of it a hybrid at 3/11d a time to please us. I hope people who buy these do not then start boasting they are collecting wood carvings. Real African carving with its virile phallic emphasis and thundering ritual would sicken many Westerners. Among the finest African carvings are the erectile phalluses made by the Yoruba and other tribes, and used for the indoctrination of virgins. But they would not look very 'nice' on the store counters. Yet they spell Africa with greater emphasis than those picturebook gazelles.

FOUR

A good day, working alone on a piece of oak with an Income Tax Demand lying crumpled on the floor where I threw it on receipt. I want to fashion a miniature screen along the lines of Winchester or Chester, but my error – which I have pigheadedly refused to acknowledge all along – is in trying to scale down from 10 ft.×20 ft or so to a one-foot square. The originals are grandiose, a paean of praise in themselves, and it is foolish to try and re-create them in portable proportions. But how good the oak is! It comes away briskly from the tools in curling or edge-shaped chips, and the revealed surface is always so uniform and satisfying. One thing you have to watch out for is the tool. If it is very sharp – as it should be for any wood – it will run on. Carving floriation is almost surgical in procedure. It is a good idea to work towards a down-cut made beforehand, and to use a light-weight mallet. Although the oak is hard and staunch, you should not be ham-fisted when it comes to detail. If you do take off a piece which is already carved, and the break is a straight one, it can be stuck on again. The new adhesives are very efficient, and they work fast in contrast to the old glueing methods. But even if nobody else notices it, the carver knows it is there.

It is common enough to feel slightly dissatisfied with everything you carve. I understand that this same feeling pervades creative writing, painting and music. It is hard to believe it of music, the highest of the arts. But once you feel smug and satisfied, you are lost.

FIVE

The set of religious reliefs, all small and compact, in Bangor Cathedral, North Wales, come from Oberammergau, I think. Although they are reliefs, the figures are almost dimensional, and they stand out with some boldness. Nobody seems to clean or oil them, and the wood has gone dull since they were presented. The expressions on the faces are amusing, for the carver created definite personalities for the Apostles, and the same characterization peeps out of each face. Set on the walls at eye level round the building, they are rather lost, and being of dark wood they are missed by many tourists.

SIX

Alceo Dossena, the Italian art forger and king of technique, who died in poverty in 1937, has fascinated me for many years. He seems to have been self-taught, but he could freely fabricate anything in the Renaissance style. During a lifetime of creating masterpieces, some of them derivatives rather than copies, he was poorly treated by the dealer-leeches who took his handiwork and sold it for thousands of times more than they paid him. Apart from working in stone, he did a number of wood carvings, including a Madonna after Simone Martini (1285–1344), and in 1921 the 'Savelli Tomb' offered to Ellen Frick, the collector. But the sale failed, because she had the dealer's story of a ruined church containing the tomb investigated, and the work was traced back to Dossena, who died without a lira to his name. The master craftsman was no more. I found a photograph of him at work the other day. Handsome and grey-haired in a rumpled lounge suit, he was at work on one of his own fakes. He looked very shy.

SEVEN

I have been looking at a half-rotted tree trunk from which it would be possible to carve a towering nude about eight feet tall. What I really want is the outer shell with the inner heartwood fallen out. But what to do with it when it is carved? Our ceilings are too low for a piece of this size. We could always move into an older, roomier house. My wife listens to my suggestions, smiling faintly and agreeing. We have pulled up our roots so often. I would like to live in Andorra with the smugglers. But now that the baby is almost born we must try to be static. Until he arrives we refer to him as Worthington. I hope he wants to carve wood or stone.

EIGHT

This is written two months later, and the baby is born – a girl we have called Ruth Ernestine. My father was Ernest, and he was a Coventry craftsman. Many girls make fine carvers, so there is still some hope in my heart.

THE END

and

THE BEGINNING

The pen and ink drawings which are included in this section are by Roger Parmiter from the author's reference sketches, collected over a period from many different cultures. They are not intended as dogmatic exercises, but should act as suggestions for carvings. The majority are capable of extension and elaboration, others call for simplification before they can lend themselves to carving treatment. All, however, share one common factor – they are interesting in line, form and general design.

90 A section from an ancient
Peruvian vase. The powerful rounded
treatment of the features suggests a
carving in teak.

91 The Mother and Child theme is
capable of many different variations.
This was derived from 'Family Group'
done in bronze for the Prudential
Assurance Company's office in
Montreal, Canada. Granted, this may
seem ambitious for the wood carver,
but it is included for the unusual
treatment of the head and the line of
the figure.

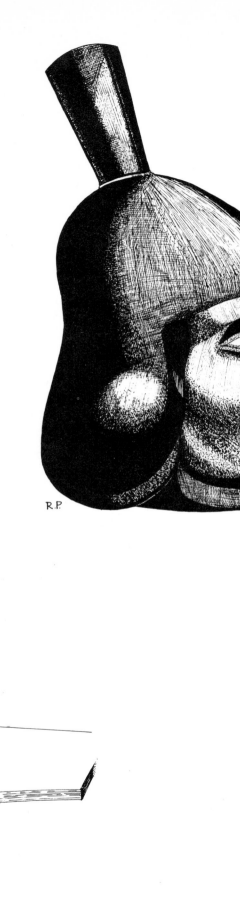

92　*Relief on the Mardith Gate of Tiahuanaco, done in wood. This form of 'primitive' treatment has its own sophistication, and if interpreted in contemporary terms can provide the basis of decorative relief panels.*

175

93 Horseman of Kafiristan, north
eastern Afghanistan. The Kafirs, living
in the high valleys of the Hindu Kush
mountains, do not possess horses, and
seldom see any. This wooden statue
stands 6½ ft high and has a singular
majesty.

94 Fragment of an enamel bas-relief
from Susa. Here again, this type of
design lends itself to carving in relief
for the richness of the decoration.

176

95   *Girl with stringed instrument from a mural painting at Thebes, Egypt. It has a 'modern' look to it and would adapt well for light relief carving.*

96   *From a Greek dish; a youthful head with dolphins playing round the rim.*

97   Inevitably, every carver has in his
mind a certain design, or figure, which
is slated for development. I am
fascinated by the curve, and combine
this with the most carved figure of all –
the Crucified Christ. Discerning
readers will see a little of Salvador
Dali's great experiment in perspective,
using the same motif. In my version
the entire figure is composed of
curves, often one on top of the other.
The obvious choice of wood for this is
English oak.

178

R.P.

R.P. 99

R.P.

R.P.

BIRDS AND BEASTS

98 *Eagle motif from a coat of arms carved in stone from the Palazzo Feroni, Italy. For hundreds of years wood carvers have executed coats of arms and heraldic devices, and this one would be a good starting point in view of the head of the bird and the treatment of the plumage.*

99 *Cornerpiece from the tomb of Cardinal Ximenez. A florid treatment of the heraldic bird, full of graceful line, and suggestive of carving, although the original is in stone.*

100 *Krubock (beaker) belonging to Prince John III. The cockerel is a recurring motif in traditional and contemporary art, and this one has a number of carving applications.*

101 *Bronze knocker from the door of St Mark's, Venice. The bar running through the mouth forms a ring to lift the head, but in this drawing it has been cut through in order to show the formation of the mouth. The design has so much strength that it automatically suggests a treatment in hard wood in order to do full justice to the supporting planes of the head.*

0

101

102

103

104

102   A marble fragment from Rome,
probably a griffon. Although there is
something faintly horrific about this,
it has some fascinating swirling lines
and would lend itself to wood carving.

103   Another familiar motif in all art,
the owl. This drawing was derived
from an interpretation in mural ceramics
with inlaid glazes by Renate Rhein.

104   A particularly ingenious design
featuring in ceiling ornament from
ancient Memphis, Egypt. Note the
treatment of the wing feathers under
the main body of the bird.

105   Gold brooch in the form of an
eagle. Fifth century.

105

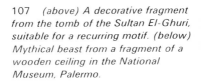

107 *(above) A decorative fragment from the tomb of the Sultan El-Ghuri, suitable for a recurring motif. (below) Mythical beast from a fragment of a wooden ceiling in the National Museum, Palermo.*

108 *Two designs from Ancient Greece. The galley (top) uses the curve in the dolphins, the prow of the vessel and the sails. It would be suited to light relief carving. The head (below) has the same kind of curve utilization, and again suggests a design for a relief carving. The galley is from a painted terracotta dish, and the head is Zeus, from Olympia.*

182

B

109 (A) *Norman Shield.* (B) *Plate from angle column of the Mauricius Shrine in Cologne.* 1180 A.D. (C) *Eagle from the hilt of a tenth-century sword.*

A

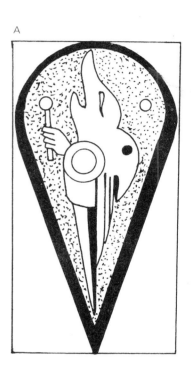

C

R

183

110   *A seventh-century horse harness piece from Vendel, Uppsala, Sweden. The original is in gilded bronze inlaid with garnets. It suggests some delicate carving in soft wood, finely stained and polished.*

111   *An ornamental butterfly from an antique porcelain plate.*

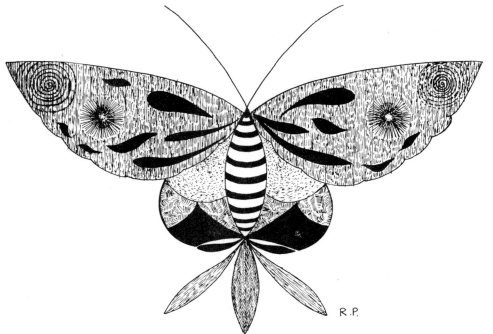

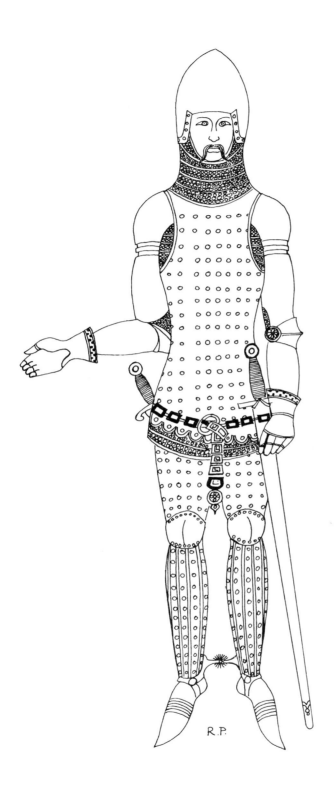

R.P.

112A *Detail from the Abbot's Barn, Glastonbury. (top)*
B *Knight from the tombstone in Ingham Church, Norfolk. (centre)*
C *Patterns from ornaments in Kinfeelstein Castle. (bottom pair)*

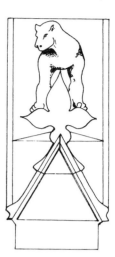

113 *An example of geometrical design based on the square.*

R.P.

114 *A Celtic Shield. The drawing is based on a shield dating to the first century B.C., found in the River Thames. Similar finds have been made in France, Spain and north Italy, evidence of a Celtic migration from the Upper Danube into western Europe between the seventh and third centuries B.C. The geometric design, which lends itself well to wood carving uses curvilinear motifs, circles and spirals, and is notable for its lack of monotony. The original is in bronze and may be seen in the British Museum, London.*

R.P.

Bibliography

It is quite difficult to recommend books for carvers of all ages, because this is primarily a visual process, and you do far more looking than reading. But the following titles are useful.

Speltz, Alexander: *Styles of Ornament.* Published originally in Germany, 1904. Available in cheap paperback edition, Dover. Well worth the money for the thousands of examples of anthropological, architectural and other ornament which it contains. The only drawback is the plates, which would benefit from re-drawing for heavier emphasis.

Howard, F. E. and **Crossley, F. H.**: *English Church Woodwork.* Batsford, 1917. A good reference work for ecclesiastical ornament.

Eaton, Allen H.: *Handicrafts of the Southern Highlands.* Russell Sage Foundation, New York, 1937.

Handbook of the Ethnographical Collections, 2nd ed. British Museum, 1925. A very useful guide to the art of other cultures.

188